Human Connection at Work

How to use the principles of Nonviolent Communication in a professional way

LIV LARSSON

friare **LIV**

www.friareliv.se/eng

Published by
Friare Liv
Mjösjölidvägen 477
946 40 Svensbyn
Telefon: 0911- 24 11 44
info@friareliv.se
www.friareliv.se

Author: Liv Larsson
Translator: Liv Larsson and Sara Hellsten.
Proofreading: Peggy Smith
Belinda Poropudas
Cover & Layout: Kay Rung
Cover picture: Istockphotos

ISBN Printed edition 978-91-87489-56-3
ISBN ePub 978-91-87489-57-0

Content

Exercises

Preface

Connecting with others is an art that can be continually refined. A variety of components affect the process of connecting with people and this book describes some of them. Above all, the focus is on how communication, in thought, word and action, affects situations where people are connecting. It is this "software" in the connection between people that I have experience of and want to share.

This book is an attempt to answer some questions that people from different working groups, teams, professions, associations and management groups have asked me during courses about connection that I have led. Since each person and group is unique, the answers in this book are sometimes more general than they would be if we were addressing a specific situation. My hope is that they can give you hints and inspiration for solutions in your own situations.

I have read many inspiring books on how to create connection and on how to treat customers, guests and fellow workers in an authentic, respectful, and honest way. Although they have often inspired me, I have at the same time been frustrated by a lack of concrete tools to work with and the possibility to practice in advance, situations that are challenging and tend to repeat themselves. My hope is that the combination of inspiration and practical tools in this book will help create an even more meaningful connection with people in whatever situation you find yourself. Practice makes perfect and the world is full of people to practice with.

For the english edition of this book I feel a deep gratitude towards Sara Hellsten, Belinda Poropudas and Peggy Smith. They have helped me with the translation and in finding words that are not fully translatable in a manner that I appreciate from the bottom om my heart. To feel supported in that way is an experience that I wish for everyone.

Chapter 1

To See and Be Seen

As a teenager I once visited Stockholm and experienced a connecting situation that affected me deeply. I took a bus out to a market place in Stockholm and although it was a standard city bus, the driver told us passengers about the buildings and areas we passed. We passed several museums - ethnographical, technical, maritime and historical museums, and he continued to merrily talk about all the sites that existed along the road. He warmly welcomed everyone who stepped on the bus, welcoming them without seeming obtrusive, and saying thank you and goodbye to everyone who got off. Although he addressed his attention to everyone, not just to me, I felt special. It was as if he were my personal guide on my journey through Stockholm. This experience of feeling special and important made the trip an experience I vividly remember thirty years later.

On the other hand, the feeling of being important can easily and quickly change. One of my friends used to go to a particular hairdresser who somehow made him feel special. He always left with a small bag of hair products he had bought from her. Then one day he met another man coming out of "his" hairdresser's place with the same type of bag. My friend's first impulse was to change hairdressers, because the experience of being special and important had disappeared for him. That is how important it is for us to have a connection and a sense of being seen as a human being.

Each situation is unique, but even so, there are some general components affecting all connections and that is what this book is about.

REFLECTION:
Think of a time when somebody connected to you in a way that you appreciated?
What did this person say or do?
What can you learn from this situation?

Created for Communication

"All real life is meeting."
MARTIN BUBER

Humans are social animals, created to live in community, connected to others. We have the power to contribute to one another's well-being and we are mutually dependent on the people and nature around us. We may have heard about treating others the way we want to be treated, and we can also consider that not everybody appreciates the same treatment. But we all have needs to experience acceptance, respect, and belonging.

Some years ago I wrote a book on intimate relationships. When I began writing this book, I realized that many of the same principles that work in an intimate relationship actually work in a professional setting as well. Principles such as really seeing the human being in everyone is of course important in personal relationships, but also in a relationship with a client, patient, student, guest or co-worker. As humans we feel good when we see that other people feel good. When we manage to contribute to another person's well-being, we feel happy ourselves. If we enjoy what we do and it is in line with our values, it becomes easier for us to contribute to the people we meet.

Research indicates that loneliness is a major threat to our health, with some researchers arguing that loneliness is more fatal than smoking and obesity. Persons who have few or no personal relationships are less prone to care for their health and have lower mental resilience[1]. We are social beings that need others to thrive

---

1. www.expressen.se/halsa/1.2234319/ensamhet-kan-gora-dig-sjuk

and as humans we enjoy contributing to other human beings.

Sometimes we enjoy solitude, but exclusion or a feeling of involuntary isolation is something else entirely. Involuntary exclusion is not good for us, which is something most people know intuitively and therefore connection with other people becomes a very central part of our lives.

One of my friends worked at a bar where one evening a man who was very drunk came in. My friend refused to serve him more alcohol, stating that he was already drunk. The man became very angry and left the bar yelling. A few nights later my friend saw the same man enter the bar and, after looking around, approaching the bar counter with determined steps. My friend was afraid, but the man wanted only to shake his hand and thank him for refusing to serve him more alcohol at their earlier meeting. The man told him that one of his best friends had passed away some time ago. This friend had often told him "unpleasant truths," much in the same manner as the "no" my friend had given him. After his friend's death he had felt really lonely and desperate. He had been unable to mourn, and instead had drowned his grief with alcohol. But finally through the anger stimulated by my friends "no," he had found the tears and embraced his grief. He had cried through the night and woken up with a new sense of peace and acceptance for what had happened. Now he was grateful for the support he had received. Understanding is important, but in order to lead to true connection, understanding needs to be accompanied by tender, and often courageous, honesty. Through my friend's "no" this man was able to connect with his own grieve over the loss of his own friend, who had so often connected with him by speaking the truth.

Connection occurs both from being listened to but also from hearing and taking in what the other person needs and wants. An encounter that we find upsetting can create stress and stay with us for a long time. After being yelled at, a heightened level of tension can remain for a week or even longer. The stress of unresolved conflicts with a guest, customer or employee may contribute to further challenging situations, because we easily miss signals from around us when we are under pressure. When we have experienced a connection that did not work, we can withdraw in the future and thus end up with more problems. We can start reading problems and hostility into situations where they actually don't exist. Therefore, it is time well invested both for the individual and for the organization as a whole to look into how to create satisfying interactions and connection between people. Wanting to feel connection and to experience cooperation is deeply human.

Seeing the Human

The core message of this book is how we can "see the human being" behind a person's actions and behind what he or she says. To "see" someone may seem easy. But at the same time it seems to be the most challenging to do so when it is the most needed. When people threaten, blame or demand something of us, it is easy to become "infected" by their attitude and fight back with the same weapons they are using in trying to defend ourselves. That rarely ends in a satisfying outcome. I found inspiration in Byron Katie's statement, "Defense is the first act of war".[2]

Seeing people as human beings also involves seeing oneself as a human being and not as a function, profession or title. It means daring to drop the facade and be "genuine" and interested in another human being.

To be able to see others, we need a sense of having been seen ourselves. It does not need to be by a specific person, but maybe by a co-worker, boss, friend or mentor with whom we can "refuel" our willingness to connect.

Connecting with people is based on both being clear about what they want and need, but also about what we want and need. In order to do our job, we need to learn how the human factor affects different situations. This includes the ability to repair con-

---

2. www.squidoo.com/byronkatieandthework

nections that have taken a blow.

What we call the people we meet affects how we respond to them. We create an image within our mind that can either help us or prevent us from connecting with them. Do we call them customers, guests, patients or students? Do we call them visitors or users? Do we call them by name, or do we think of them as a role or a function? The doctor? The priest? The maid? Does what we call them make us superior or inferior, or does it create distance? When I call myself a patient, I have noticed that I might agree to things I regret later because I've seen myself as inferior. If I see myself as a customer or a guest, I often find it easier to stand up for my needs and requests.

In the rest of this book I have often chosen to call the people we meet "customers". To call someone a customer helps me find the attitude I want to have when I connect with someone and see how I can serve him or her. Some other word might work better for you, so please exchange the word as you continue to read to what is best for you.

REFLECTION:

What do you call the people you meet at work?
Customers? Guests? Patients? Students? Visitors?
How does what you call them affect your relationship with them?

A customer can be described as someone who has expectations of a person or an organization. By that definition, there are customers in the vast majority of organizations. We may also want to ask ourselves what Machiavelli asked himself a long time ago:

"The question is, then, do we try to make things easy on ourselves or do we try to make things easy on our customers, whoever they may be?"
NICCOLO MACHIAVELLI, 1513

I Don't See You - My Image Of You Got in the Way

When we experience that a connection with someone does not feel comfortable, we often begin to make judgments. If we do not get what we need in a relationship, many of us have learned to deal with that disappointment by focusing on whose fault it is. We start to look for flaws in others or in ourselves. For example, it is easy to think of someone as lazy if we do not get help with a problem in time; or as "greedy" if he or she does not want to share what he or she has; or "selfish" if we do not experience the care we want. When our ideas do not seem to reach others, we may begin to think of ourselves as uninteresting or stupid.

If someone calls us lazy, we might begin to think of ourselves in the same way. We may begin to over-compensate to prove otherwise, which may increase our stress because we do more than we actually have the energy to do.

Labels and static ideas contribute to people feeling locked into a role and sometimes into a pattern of behavior. It can lead both to attempts to prove the opposite of how we are labeled and to self-fulfilling prophecies.

If we think of someone as dominant, we might pay particular attention to when that person wants to make a decision about something, more often than when someone else shows the same behavior. I've seen groups of people make fun of a person when he says he wants to listen to what others would like to do, because they have so much pain from previous situations when that person did not listen or ask for their consideration. Someone might say, "Have you taken a charm course?" or "What do you want from me now?"

I have seen how persons labeled as lazy, when trying to be involved in projects, are hampered by comments such as:

"Sure, and what will happen when you get tired of this?!"

or "Are you really sure you want to sign up for this?"

These kinds of comments are not very supportive for a person that perhaps is shy or unclear about how she or he wants to engage with others. The people saying these kinds of things are most likely carrying some disappointment from previous projects with this person, or have heard labels given to this person from others that makes them want to be sure that they know this person will really be engaged.

These kinds of comments trap people in a particular behavior that is not supportive for anyone. Another situation where we might get stuck in labels and static images of someone is when we see the person as a function or a role, rather than as the human being she or he is.

REFLECTION:
During a week, write down labels, positive and negative, that you put on people you meet. Be attentive to any possible judgments that often recur and take the time to try to understand what they have to say about what you need. Try not to censor but also do not express your labels out loud to the person you are judging.

Many years ago, I led a training for the staff of a bank and noticed that I had lots of presumptions about them. When I got to the bank, and met the staff, I found them to be very human and a warm bunch of people. This helped me recognize and then let go of the "enemy images" I had created in my mind. Sometimes you get help when you need it the most! If for example, they had been nervous or stressed, and not as cordial in their welcome as they were, I would have thought that my presumptions were accurate. My thoughts that everyone working in a bank is cold and impersonal could have contaminated our encounter, become a self-fulfilling prophecy and made our contact difficult. When after a few training sessions, I embarrassedly told the staff about my prejudices, many said that they recognized my thoughts. They actually had the same prejudices themselves about those who work at a bank, even though their daily reality proved that this was not real.

If we have learned that it is wrong to judge, it is easy to judge others if they express themselves in ways that we consider to be judgmental. We might call them narrow-minded or cold. And when we discover that we now are the ones judging, perhaps we judge ourselves for doing that. It becomes a never-ending carousel of judgments and comparisons. For me, the way out has been through finding the needs behind the judgments, whether it is me or other people who are judging. To do that, I need to admit to myself that I judge and have prejudices. The next step is to find what it is that I need and want that leads me to comparing and judging.

A Place Beyond Prejudices

Beyond ideas of right and wrong there is a place,
I will meet you there.
RUMI, PERSIAN 1200 CENTURY POET

How people respond to others if they believe that the person they meet is a doctor or if they believe that she or he is part of the cleaning staff has been studied in several research projects. In some of these studies subjects said that they treat everyone equally and are not influenced by appearances or titles. But when they were observed, the observers saw that they did behave differently depending on whom they met. For example, did they shake hands or not, did they look down or did they look the other person in the eyes, did they respond very briefly or did they say a lot when they met someone.

The first step to really seeing people is realizing that we have prejudices and that we will probably never get rid of this habit of evaluating others. When we recognize that, then we can recognize the difference between learned prejudices and the actual human being that stands before us. If we refuse to acknowledge our learned prejudices, we risk unconsciously acting in ways that will block connection. If we instead recognize our judgments, we can use them as a signal that we need something.

When we think of a person as his or her title or role, it is easy to get stuck in ideas about how for example, a doctor, a priest or a truck driver should behave. Sure, it is convenient to use labels sometimes, but if we confuse people and specific encounters with our preconceived ideas about a particular profession or role, we risk missing important parts of a human encounter.

During our trainings on how to connect with people in the work place, I have seen that most people know a lot about what's important when it comes to connecting to people, whether it is customers, guests or fellow human beings. The hard part usually is to access that knowledge when it is most needed. When we become stressed our autonomic nervous system kicks in, and our reaction is "fight or flight". This stone-age reaction is triggered when we think we are in danger. Therefore it is important to practice how to handle different situations beforehand, so that we can manage reactions before they get out of hand in the actual situation. In the same way that athletes practice before challenging championship competitions, it is possible to exercise the ability to communicate and think before important meetings with people. But we also need to remember that most of us have well-programmed prejudices that we may never have gotten rid of. The good news is that we can cultivate new ways to act that can help us to manage avoiding being driven by these prejudices when we discover them, and remain "the captain of our own ship." Put simply, one could say that establishing a functional connection is about being present with those we want to connect to and to listen to them and to what they want. In our trainings, when we deal with the subject of how to be able to see even "difficult" individuals, we often get this question:

"But how do you do that, how do I put myself in the other person's shoes? I understand that it would be good to really see this human being, but I only see a difficult person that I mostly want to get rid of as quickly as possible?"

When it comes to human connection there are no simple solutions or "techniques" that will work at all times. But being present with the other person often makes a big difference. There are various things we can do to stay present.

If we want to understand someone else's reactions, it is helpful to find a "common denominator". And I do not mean that we need to share an interest or even that we have to have experienced the same thing as the other person. We can find this common denominator by asking in which ways can we recognize ourselves in what the other person wants and needs?

When we focus on what we know we all have in common – human needs - it is easier to find ways to really create connection and understanding between us.

It can be challenging at first to connect with people on that level if we have not actively practiced it. Many of us have received extensive training in how to argue, or to find out who is right and who is wrong. The most common reason why we find it difficult to connect is that we ourselves need to be seen and listened to in order to be able to see and listen to the other person.

The simplest and most useful way to see another person is to approach him or her on the need level. An important part of what makes us human is that we all share the same needs. We all long for some basic qualities in life, although we strive to attain them in many different ways. Here are some words for the needs I see that all people have in common:

Freedom, choice, community, love, care, respect, acceptance, to be seen and heard, meaning, stimulation, rest, intimacy, food, water and sleep.

Imagine that you judge a person for behaving irresponsibly. If you focus on your analysis of him or her, it will be difficult to "see the person" behind what he or she has done. However, if you focus on the needs he or she was trying to meet while doing what he or she did, perhaps the need for acceptance or being seen, you can recognize yourself in the other person. Connecting with their needs does not mean we are OK with what they have done, but it will make it easier for us to connect with them. We "walk in the other person's shoes" for a while to get a chance to understand their intentions.

When we recognize the needs behind what someone does, we can create connection and communicate in a constructive way. We can express what we want the person to do differently without the person having to give up his or her needs. Needs can be supported and met in many ways.

If we have trouble understanding what human needs this person might be experiencing, we can focus on what she or he feels. Feelings are like the fragrance of a flower, but it is not the actual flower. However, the fragrance can lead us to a guess at what kind of flower it is. When we guess about how someone feels, we might ask ourselves - what do I usually need, long for, want or take an interest in when I feel that way?

Sometimes it is hard to believe that the other person is driven by human needs. Our enemy images make it challenging to see them as human. And if we get caught in the idea that it is our duty to help the person, this becomes even more challenging. When we do something because it is our duty, we often lose the focus on what is human. To get beyond this, we need the ability to listen to ourselves first and find our needs behind our judgments of others. When we are at peace with ourselves, it is easier to really hear others even if they express themselves through criticism or demands.

My greatest source of inspiration on how to listen is Nonviolent Communication (NVC)[3]. It has struck me that complaints rarely seem to be about what people say they are dissatisfied with. Therefore, it is a great gift to be able to stop and listen to the person who complains about something. The conversation below, from Marshall Rosenberg's book Nonviolent Communication, A Language of Life, shows us how valuable it is to neither agree - that the physiotherapist is doing a poor job - nor to argue against that, when we really want to show someone that we are listening.

A patient had just been diagnosed with an advanced stage of lung cancer. The following scene at his home, involving the pa-

3 www.cnvc.org or www.friareliv.se/eng

tient, his wife, and a visiting nurse, represents a last opportunity for him to connect emotionally with his wife and discuss his dying before being admitted to the hospital. The wife begins the conversation with the nurse by complaining about the physical therapist that was part of the home health care team assigned to her husband's care.

Wife: She's a bad therapist.

Nurse: (listening with empathy to what the wife is feeling and wanting) Are you feeling annoyed and wanting to see a different quality of care?

Wife: She doesn't do anything. She made him stop walking when his pulse got high.

Nurse: (continuing to hear the wife's feelings and wants) Is it because you want your husband to get better that you're scared if the physical therapist doesn't push him, he won't get stronger?

Wife: (starting to cry) Yes, I'm so scared!

Nurse: Are you scared of losing him?

Wife: Yes, we've been together so long.

Nurse: (listening for other feelings behind the fear) Are you worrying about how you would feel if he dies?

Wife: I just can't imagine how I am going to live without him. He's always been there for me. Always.

Nurse: So you're sad when you think of living without him?

Wife: There is no one else besides him. He's all I have, you know.

My daughter won't even talk to me.

Nurse: It sounds like when you think of your daughter, you feel frustrated because you wish you had a different relationship with her.

Wife: I wish I did, but she is such a selfish person. I don't know why I even bothered having kids. A lot of good it does me now!

Nurse: Sounds to me like you might be somewhat angry and disappointed because you want more support from the family during your husband's illness.

Wife: Yes, he's so sick; I don't know how I am going to get through this alone. I haven't anyone . . . not even to talk to, except with you here . . . now. Even he won't talk about it. . . . Look at him!
(Husband remains silent and impassive.) He doesn't say anything!

Nurse: Are you sad, wishing the two of you could support each other and feel more connected?

Wife: Yes. (She pauses, then makes a request.) Talk to him the way you talk to me.

Nurse: (wishing to clearly understand the need that is being addressed behind the wife's request) Are you wanting him to be listened to in a way that helps him express what he's feeling inside?

Wife: Yes, yes, that's exactly it! I want him to feel comfortable talking and I want to know what he is feeling.

Using the nurse's guess, the wife was able to first become aware of what she wanted and then find the words to articulate it. This was a key moment: often it is difficult for people to identify what they want in a situation, even though they may know what they don't want. We see how a clear request; "Talk to him the way you talk to me", is a gift that empowers the other person. The nurse was then able to act in a way she knew to be in harmony with the wife's wishes. This altered the atmosphere in the room, as the nurse and the wife could now "work together," both in a compassionate mode.

Nurse: (turning to the husband) How do you feel when you hear what your wife has shared?

Husband: I really love her.

Nurse: Are you glad to have an opportunity to talk about this with her?

Husband: Yes, we need to talk about it.

Nurse: Would you be willing to say how you are feeling about the cancer?

Husband: (after a brief silence) Not very good.

The words good and bad are often used to describe feelings when people have yet to identify the specific emotion they are experiencing. Expressing his feelings more precisely would help this patient with the emotional connection he was seeking with his wife.

Nurse: (encouraging him to move toward more precision)
Are you scared about dying?

Husband: No, not scared. (Notice the nurse's incorrect guess does not hamper the continued flow of dialogue.)

Nurse: (Because this patient isn't able to verbalize his internal experience easily, the nurse continues to support him in the process.) Do you feel angry about dying?

Husband: No, not angry.

Nurse: (At this point, after two incorrect guesses, the nurse decides to express her own feelings.) Well, now I'm puzzled about what you may be feeling, and wonder if you can tell me.

Husband: I reckon, I'm thinking how she'll do without me.

Nurse: Oh, are you worried she may not be able to handle her life without you?

Husband: Yes, worried she'll miss me.

Nurse: (She is aware that dying patients often hang on due to worry over those they are leaving behind, and sometimes need reassurance that loved ones can accept their death before they can let themselves go.) Do you want to hear how your wife feels when you say that?

Husband: Yes.

Here the wife joined the conversation; in the continued presence of the nurse, the couple began to express themselves openly to each other.
In this dialogue, the wife began with a complaint about the physical therapist. However, after a series of exchanges during which she felt emphatically received, she was able to determine that what she really sought was a deeper connection with her husband during this critical stage of their lives.[4]

---

[4] Rosenberg, Marshall (2007) Nonviolent Communication, A Language for life. Puddle Dancer.

Beyond Appearance

One of my friends was giving a training to some salesmen. At one point he asked them to do an experiment with him – to go into a number of shops in the city dressed in two different ways - one week in suits and another week as shabbily as possible.

When they entered the shop dressed in a suit or a dress, they immediately caught the clerk's attention, and when they came in jeans and T-shirts, they needed to ask for help themselves.

They did not, of course, feel especially welcome in the latter case and did not want to continue as customers in the store. My partner (who is a Swedish male) likes home furnishing and housewares. This is nothing I am interested in, but still, in most of the stores that sell such things, the staff turns their attention to me rather than to my partner. Correspondingly, many car salesmen have turned to my partner, when it is me who is looking for a new car. As soon as we look at someone, we make a rapid analysis of the person. We do not need much information to form an opinion of someone. Without any effort, our subconscious creates an image and interpretation of an idea about what we perceive. One of the first things we check out is gender – is this a man or a woman? Nothing wrong with that, but if we believe we do not treat men and women differently and we actually do, it can get us into trouble. Other categories are rich, poor, smart, dangerous etc. In many studies, including one at Princeton University in the United States from 2006, subjects were shown unknown faces for a brief moment, sometimes for as little as a tenth of a second.[5] Then the subjects were asked to answer different questions. Did they think that the person was popular? Could he or she be trusted? Was he or she trustworthy? Was he or she competent? The experiment showed, that even though the subjects got to look at the same faces once more and for a longer time, they rarely changed their first assessment. They rather became more confident in their opinions. What we think we know about an unknown person's skills only

5. Ezra, Emmanuel (2010), Det goda mötet. Norstedts

by looking at his or her face, of course, also influences our contact with the person. Even though we want to see ourselves as rational, we are influenced by people's appearance and how we evaluate them based on it. If we deny that we make interpretations based on our prejudices, we are in trouble. However, when we recognize that we are judging someone for being "a slob", another for being "artistic" and a third for being "indecisive," and realize that our judgments are just judgments and not the truth about these people, we can choose more freely how we want to act towards them.

Once a person taking one of our trainings expressed a desire to learn not to relate to people based on how they looked. She had previously had some troubles due to this, both when she had said "yes," and when she had said "no," based on how she judged a person by appearance. "But how do you do it?" she asked as soon as I brought up the subject.

The first step is to become aware that we judge a person after even just a few seconds of meeting or seeing them. Maybe even before we actually meet them, based on their name, title, or anything someone else has said about them. But remember - behind each judgment there are beautiful needs, so listen extra carefully to what is going on inside you when you have strong judgments based on someone's appearance. For example, if you judge someone for being "sloppy", then maybe you are worried because you have a need for clarity, safety and cooperation. If you judge someone for being "indecisive", you may feel frustrated because you need support and trust. One of the worst things we can do is to pretend that we do not make judgments, because then the judgments will control us in an unconscious way.

To go deeper in exploring how you can transform labels into observations, feelings, needs and requests use the exercise on page 154.

Alert!

Look out for situations when you use the verb "to be" when talking about others. When you say "he or she is ..." something, it is a sign that you probably have mixed an interpretation into what this person can be observed doing or what we have heard them saying.

This is also true when we say "you should be more...", "she should be less ...," or "what if she would just ...". Use the verb "to be" (whether it's you or someone else using it) as a wake-up call. Evaluate the situation instead of going on autopilot and make sure to separate facts from the interpretations of facts.

Professional = Inhuman?

Many participants in our trainings on how to connect with people have raised questions about balancing "the professional role," with "being human". To my frustration, I have heard people describing someone as professional, meaning that the person does not show their human side.

I think we can be human and professional at the same time. Not that we need to be best friends with everyone, but I would go so far as to say that being professional is about showing that we are also human. For me the bus driver who "guided" me through Stockholm (see page 9) was not less professional because he did it, but rather more so. I felt in that case that I was not just a "passenger" but also a human being he was helping to have a good day as well as a pleasant trip.

Freedom of choice is, of course, very important here. We need to feel that we can decide ourselves how personal or open we want to be. And at the same time we need to take into account what we also believe serves the person we are connected to.

People unknown to us may not want to hear our whole life

story, but they might be interested in our well-being. If you read this and are thinking that you will try to be more human as a kind of "technique," it probably will not give the effect you are hoping for. What I am suggesting is that we connect with others with a genuine intention to be of use, without exposing the parts of ourselves we do not want to show.

If people do not see you as a human being with the same feelings and needs as they have, but only as a role, it can lead to a kind of communication that complicates your connection.

Someone I know shared a situation on Face book. People thought they were helping by sharing advice. But even if they are clearly wanting to support her, the advice probably did not help her much. The advice may instead support her to react in a way that will make it harder for her to get what she needs.

Aida: Got the wrong 'compensation from the social security'. Only a third of the usual, just in time for Christmas. It feels like a good start ... not!

Then Aida gets the following suggestions and comments.

1. They are hopeless! They never get things rights.

2. What the hell? Call them!!! And tell them that they are idiots and to immediately ...

If Aida (or someone else in her situation) listens to this advice, it is likely that she gets herself worked up when she makes the call to the social security office to find out what has happened.

The First Contact

At the core of a functioning and satisfactory connection is the ability to "seeing the human being". When we show someone we are interested in listening to him or her, it becomes easier for the other person to feel heard and seen. It does not take any longer to pay attention to a person that we meet, than it takes not do it. The difference is in your presence and willingness to pay attention to the other person.

In some cultures, people shake hands when they meet a new person. In others, they look each other in the eye and introduce themselves, or kiss each other on the cheek. Still in others, people put one hand on their heart while shaking hands. In some cultures, people are "straight on" in the connection and in others they let the visitor take the initiative. But even within the same culture there are large individual differences of how we take the first steps to connect. It is a mistake to believe that a whole ethnic group prefer to be greeted in a certain way but they might be familiar with a certain way.

Although I have heard people say, "The Swedish way to greet is to shake hands," I do not recognize myself in it. I did not grow up in a culture where people were shaking hands, except in formal contexts. Because I know that many people often feel welcomed and seen by shaking hands, I do it when I think it helps.

I went to the U.S. to attend a conference. The first morning I sat alone at my table in the hotel restaurant and ate breakfast. Some Americans came up to my table and asked if they could sit with me and I said it was okay. Then all shook hands and introduced themselves. It took me a few days to get used to all the handshaking especially since it was connected to the simple act of sitting at the same breakfast table.

Having worked in both Thailand and Sri Lanka, cultural differences toward physical contact has become clear to me. Because I am used to hugging someone I know when I meet them again, at least when I have not met him or her in a few months, I tried it a few times. But being met with a confused look and a stiff hug back, I realized that this was not the best way to establish connection. It was even worse because they had seen me in my role as a teacher, and you do not hug a teacher!

Shaking hands has in Thailand and other parts of Asia become a way to greet others when there are people from the West around. Otherwise, they bow with their hands in front of their heart, even when they know each other pretty well.

Visiting southern Europe the kissing on the cheeks, how many kisses, with whom, and which cheek you start with, has always been a mystery to me. Often I go through the kissing laughing. Sometimes I have missed a cheek when the person has aimed at my second cheek and kissed a mouth instead. I have often been told that the kiss should be in the air next to the cheek, and not so close as I do it. Sometimes it's two, sometimes three or four kisses that apply and I never seem to get it. Of course I'm excused with the idea that "I'm Swedish" so I do not know better.

To understand that we have different ways to make the first steps to connect is valuable when we meet people from other cultures. If others are accustomed to greeting people in a certain way, it can lead to confusion if we greet them in another way. I do not mean that we need to greet them their way but the awareness of differences can make a big difference in how we deal with their possible reactions.

In her book The Continuum Concept Jean Liedloff, wrote about her time with indigenous peoples in South America.[6] She writes among other things, about how it was to come to a new village after a few hours or days of trekking through the jungle. The first thing that happened was that one or two people came up to the travelers and showed them a place where they could relax. Shortly after, they got something to eat and drink. Only after this, the villagers started coming by, one by one, to welcome them. After a few hours they were integrated in the village.

It may seem frosty or distant to some, but I like it. It would help me to really settle, instead of being overwhelmed by new im-

6 Liedloff, Jean (1986) The Continuum Concept. Da Capo Press Inc

pressions and maybe forget half the names of the people I meet. I recognize this way of welcoming people that Liedloff describes from how it was in my grandfather's village when I was small. At anytime during the day, any of the villagers would come to pay a visit. They greeted with a brief "hello" or nothing at all. Then they often went to the wood stove where they always found a pot of hot coffee, poured themselves a cup and sat down on the sofa or at the kitchen table. Sometimes a conversation was initiated, and sometimes not. The connection was clear, and also was the care and concern about each other.

Read more about preparations for meeting new people in the section "Preparations" in Chapter 6.

Connection Has Many Components

Central to situations where we connect to others is of course contact, but also respect, to be seen, and to experience oneself as important. These are human needs and therefore they are important components to consider if we want to strengthen our ability to communicate and connect. What I mean by connection is that I strive to understand what it is that motivates you and what you need, and that you understand the same things about me. Contact in that sense, puts human needs in a central position. To focus on what is right or wrong, normal or abnormal, appropriate or inappropriate is secondary.

When we connect at the need level, we have laid the foundation for mutual understanding and with that a willingness to contribute to each other. It does not mean that we have deep and long conversations or that we will be best friends. But we can show that we are interested in that the other person gets their needs met and how we are willing contribute to that.

REFLECTION:
Who you do you think is good at making themselves understood?
Who listens in a way you like?
What can you learn from them?

Listening is Worthwhile

"As a matter of fact, have you never noticed that most conversations are simply monologues delivered in the presence of a witness?"

MARGARET MILLER

What if we, instead of saying, " let's talk about it," said - " let's sit down and listen to each other"? Surely this would invite to a different experience?!

Listening is perhaps the most important part of communication. (Someone said that maybe it's why we have two ears but only one mouth!) . If we are having a conversation where we find it difficult to listen- perhaps because we ourselves have not had the chance to be heard - there are several things we can do. First, admit to ourselves that we are actually having a hard time listening in that moment. Secondly we might say something like:

"I am finding that this situation challenging. Because I want to understand you, I would prefer that you listen to me first. I trust that it will be easier for me to hear your point of view after having expressed mine. Are you willing to start like that?"

If we have an inner conflict but don't say anything it is likely to influence conversations in a negative way. But we may face situations where it is not possible or suitable that we are listened to first. Perhaps we are meeting a guest and there is not space to express how something affects us right then. Then it is helpful to remember that our need to be heard can be supported later by a different person. I can choose to stay focused on the person who seems to be triggering me and arrange to speak to a trusted colleague later. With the colleague, make sure that it is not agreement or sympathy you get, because this can make your preconceived ideas about the third party bigger and even more difficult to let go of[7].

One thing that often works for me when I have not seen any opportunity for me to be heard, is to simply remind myself that I can be heard later, that it does not happen exactly in this moment. I sometime remind myself of the research below about the doctors that listen, to remember that in the long run it is smart to listen to complaints. I have also noticed that when I listen to somebody else, it often leads to them being willing to listen to me.

In the United States, where doctors are commonly sued, studies have shown that it is not the quality of work that predicts a law suit, but whether or not the patient and relatives felt their concerns were listened to by the doctor.

Before an important conversation, it is useful to consider what the other person might want us to understand. What do we believe is the other person's most important message? Will she or he say something that will be challenging for us to hear? What can we do to "see the human being" beyond what he or she says? What do we believe that he or she is feeling or needing?[8]

REFLECTION:
What are your "triggers"? What triggers your emotions in such a way that it is a challenge to keep listening?
Does this happen in a specific situation with a certain person?
Is there anything you can do to prepare yourself in order to not get so triggered?

This is a story I heard from a colleague:
My neighbor, a teacher, had a father visiting the classroom of the children in the first grade. He noticed a child's disappointment of not being selected as the one who would deliver today's

---

7. Read more about this on page xx at the topic,"To agree can be the worst form of support".

weather report, and said: "It's not so bad, you might be selected tomorrow." The child replied: "I'm not into problem solving. I just wanted someone to listen to me." This child seemed to have understood the power of being heard rather than trying to console, pep or cover up a hurt.

Listening in the way I suggest in this book is something different from listening to the first few sentences someone says before coming up with a solution. If you do not listen actively, it might be that the answers you come up with are based on your own preferences and not, as in the example above, the student's (or in another context, the guest's or client's) wishes and needs.

Regard listening as an investment. If you listen actively and invest time, energy and interest, it will be easier to reach connection. It will also become easier for the other person to listen to you.

REFLECTION:

If there are frequent misunderstandings in your environment, they may have been stimulated by something in your communication that you are not yet aware of. One way to find out is to ask people around you how they perceive your ability to communicate. Pay attention to how you listen to what they say: do you argue against it; claim that they are wrong; are you silent; or do you just take everything they say as the truth? The way you react provides information about your common communication patterns.

The Customer Affects The Service

A customer's way of communicating affects the services he or she receives. I'm not saying that he or she is responsible as in, "if you get bad service, you only have yourself to blame". I'm suggesting that everyone who is part of a conversation influences its progress to some extent.

Once my partner wanted to dump a broken washing machine at the garbage dump, and he arrived five minutes after closing time. He had driven a long way and really wanted to get rid of the machine. The staff was still there so he asked if there was any possibility to leave it, although he had arrived late. It was clear to him that the responsibility of being on time was his. He neither tried to convince nor force the person to let him in, he just asked and was admitted. The person who let him in said nothing when my partner thanked him for doing so. When my partner was about to drive away, the man who let him in gave him a roll of plastic bags and said, "Thank you, we are so used to people being rude or demanding that we open up even though they are late. It's nice to meet someone who takes responsibility."

The person who performs a job is of course also only human. To be treated as such invites reciprocal treatment back towards us. Being threatened, called stupid or having someone attempt to persuade us rarely leads to feeling joy in contributing to somebody.

Useful Assumptions about Human Beings

The following assumptions about people and communication can be useful when we want to connect with others. Rather than "truths", they are guidelines or sources of inspiration we can turn to when it is unclear how we want to communicate. This book is also based on "human nature" as described in these assumptions. I believe that, because we are free to make any assumptions we like about people, then why not choose some that seem to make it easier to connect.

We share have the same needs

If we can connect to what another person needs, it is easier to be of support to that person. To turn our attention to needs gives us an opportunity to see the human being, no matter how they act or express those needs.

Everyone's needs are important to take into account

If we take into account what everyone involved in a certain situation needs, it will contribute to increased trust and goodwill. When we act to try to get everyone's needs met (including our own), our relationships are characterized by mutual interest and respect. Everyone will benefit from considering everyone's needs important.

Emotions helps other connect with us

When we tell other people what we feel, it is easier for them to recognize and realize that we are human beings just like them. To distinguish what we think about a situation from what we feel makes it easier for others to understand what we need and to feel compassion.

Emotions help us understand what people need

Emotions give us clues about what people might need. When people have their needs met, they might feel joy, satisfaction, peace or excitement. When their needs are not met people have emotions such as sadness, anger, fear or anxiety.

If we connect what we feel to what we need, instead of connecting it to what we think others have done wrong, we no longer blame others. Instead of trying to get others to change, we put our effort on meeting needs, either our own, the other person's, or both.[9]

When I direct my attention to what others feel, to understand what they need, I will no longer hear criticism or feel guilt or shame.

People's actions are motivated by a wish to meet needs

Behind everything we do there is a wish to meet needs. If we are able to find strategies to meet our needs in a way that does not harm others, we prefer to do it that way. When we turn to violence, it is also an attempt to met needs (albeit in a tragic way).

People like to contribute, if it is voluntary

It is in our nature to enjoy contributing to others if we feel free from the obligation to do so. We do not like being forced because it takes away the feeling that what we are doing is a gift.

If people act in ways that do not contribute to us, we can assume that they have not figured out how they can do that while at the same time taking care of their own needs.

---

[9] Learn more about dealing with guilt and shame in a way that serves your relationships in *Anger, Guilt and Shame, Reclaiming Power and Choice* (2010) by Liv Larsson.

To distinguish observations from interpretations gives us a common reality

When our needs are not met, many of us make judgments of others. Instead of taking these judgments for the truth, we can use them as reminders of the needs behind them. When we can differentiate between our judgments of others and their actual behavior, it becomes easier to deal with conflict but also to appreciate our differences. To start with we can communicate our observations so that others know what we appreciate and not.

It is easier to deal with conflicts if we prioritize connection before solution

If we prioritize connection before finding solutions to a conflict, it will give space for development, respect and a sense of security. People want to feel more important than the "results", and are often willing to let go of their positions if they perceive themselves as important.

If we see people as free to choose how they act, it becomes easier to create connection

If we refrain from trying to control others and from using words that suggest that we "have to", "should" or "can not", we have a better opportunity to create relationships based on freedom, genuine care, compassion and respect. We see people as responsible for their choices and free to choose differently.

Even when we hear a "no" to something we have asked for we can continue to express requests. Focus on finding solutions that honor everyone's needs, not just our own, and not just those of others.

All people have the ability to experience compassion

We all have an innate ability to experience compassion. But we do not always know how we can convey it to others. Compassion is contagious, however, so when people are treated with compassion and respect, it usually evokes their own ability to relate to others in the same way.

Chapter 2

Purpose and Meaning

Before you read this chapter, take a moment to reflect on these questions:

What are the goals of the organization I am part of?
What do I want to be part of creating?

When answering the question of how we can improve our ability to connect to people, it is of great value to be clear about not only what we want to achieve in connecting with people, but also what our long-term goals are. And it is not only useful to be clear about our goals and what we can do. It is also valuable to experience the goals as our own, so that we can have joy in striving to reach them.

I visited a maternity ward where there was a large sign with the department's objectives posted in the hallway. I was impressed that the sign was placed in such a central location. Although the objectives were pretty vague, they seemed to be important for those who worked there because they were so visible. When I told a member of the staff that seeing the sign impressed me, I was surprised when she replied that she had not even thought about it hanging there, though she had worked there for two years.

In addition, she told me that she had never heard anyone in the work group talk about these objectives. It is unfortunately not uncommon that the goals and objectives of an organization or workplace are not kept relevant to the people who are meant to actualize them. The objectives of a workplace have usually been formulated by a small group of people, such as a management team, often some time ago, and they are therefore not embedded in those who are daily expected to strive in achieving them.

They may be beautiful and important goals, but they need to be "owned" to a certain degree by all the people who are charged with keeping them alive.

A clear common purpose - or the absence of it – affects a group's ability to connect to customers or guests. A positive attitude alone is superfluous unless we are convinced that what we want to achieve is important. Taking a "charm training course" rarely gives a sense of depth to our connection with others and is often judged as superficial on the part of the staff, rather than evoking confidence. To think, "things will work out" and to not be clear on where you want to go can be devastating in a situation where action and clarity about our goal are needed.

Our motivation to handle challenging situations increase when we are in alignment with our organization's goals. It makes it clear when we need to stand behind a "no" and when we can be more flexible. Providing quality service includes being clear about what we are willing to do and not do. We might also need to make it clear for the customer or the guest what is behind our yes or no.

When we tell someone about a decision we have made, it is often useful for the person affected by the decision to get some information about how the decision was reached. This minimizes the risk that he or she will take it personally, even if they do not like our decision. If he or she is not satisfied with this decision, the information about what we based the decision on gives them a possibility to question it. This in turn will determine if they appreciate how they are being treated.

Since it is central to people's motivation in the workplace to be clear about values and goals, we often begin our workplace trainings with questions about the common goals of the group. We also focus on finding out what values they feel are important. This makes it clear how each individual connection is a step in creating what they are working to achieve as a whole.

Oren Lyons, Chief of the Onondaga Nation, writes: "We are looking ahead, as is one of the first mandates given us as chiefs, to make sure and to make every decision that we make relate to the welfare and well-being of the seventh generation to come. What about the seventh generation? Where are you taking them? What will they have?"1 We can learn from this when we are caught up in achieving so much that we get stressed out. Most of us, in our stressful lives, never reflect on how our choices today will affect even our own lives tomorrow!

REFLECTION:
Which and whose values do I want to protect in my work?

One group I worked with showed reluctance in doing the communication exercises. In this particular group I had, in an effort to save time, skipped asking the question about their values. But I soon realized that we had to "rewind the tape" and take time to do this. The group was responsible for building and environmental issues in their municipality. When they had talked about their values and actual goals, it became clear that what they wanted to achieve was greater than to simply serve the citizens with permits and such. (This took no longer than half an hour!) They realized that they had a responsibility to create a city that would be functional for future generations as well. That included ensuring the protection of nature in the municipality so that future children would also have forests and lakes to enjoy.

After that, when we went on to practice connecting in various situations, their interest in learning more ways to communicate in difficult situations was much greater. Now they wanted, among other things, to learn how they could say "no" in a way that would not interfere with connecting, and how to listen more carefully to the complaints they received. They no longer experienced the training's only purpose as merely how to become clear in their communication, or to achieve more harmony in the workplace. Now they saw the training as a possibility to improve the way they wanted to contribute to their important, long-term goals.

---

1. Jump up. An Iroquois Perspective. Pp. 173, 174 in American Indian Environments: Ecological Issues in Native American History. Vecsey C, Venables RW (Editors). Syracuse University Press, New York.

Working as an educator for quite a while, I have often been a guest at various conference centers. When I arrive to attend a conference and I feel that the staff really wants to contribute, it is much easier for me to take no for an answer when I ask for something they cannot help me with. For a short period I hired a particular conference center for my courses. The owner often seemed discontented if we asked for something extra. He muttered that we were demanding, when I actually would have been okay with a clear yes or no answer to my request. As a result, I started looking for another location for my work, and also affected me in other ways. I found myself having a hard time caring about his well-being. Later on I ran into this man again. He told me that he had gone bankrupt and sold the place. To my surprise, he smiled when he said this and said:

"Managing a conference center was never what I wanted to do anyway."

Chapter 3

The Cornerstones of Communication

Use a moment to reflect on communication and misunderstandings using the question below. Use your answers as a reference while reading this chapter.

REFLECTION:
In what kind of situations do you occasionally experience misunderstanding?
What could be your part in this?
In what ways can you communicate differently in order to create more clarity and connection in these situations?

Whether we listen to complaints from a guest, want to apologize to someone, or want to open up a dialogue with someone we perceive as a challenge to understand, a large part of the result depends on our ability to communicate. Maybe we are about to meet with someone who is complaining about something we have not done, or to have a conversation with someone that our colleagues have said is a "difficult person" and we are unsure of where to start the conversation.

Just as an athlete practices difficult elements in advance, to be able to master them during a competition, we can practice how to handle difficult conversations before they take place.

There are things that make it easier to connect, that reduce stress and that allow us to minimize misunderstandings when we connect with someone.

First of all, it is useful to be clear about both what we think and what we feel. A difficult conversation is often not only difficult because of what is being said, but equally because of what is not being said or because of what someone is thinking. Beneath the surface there is something going on that also affects our dialogue with others. Our self-image might be threatened by what comes up in the conversation and we then try to defend ourselves against it. If the conversation is perceived as a conflict, there is often more intense emotions involved than what is expressed in words. Additionally there is often an internal (and sometimes external) battle over who is right and who is wrong. On top of this, there is an increased focus on power in the group at this stage. Who is wielding the power? How can I get more access to power if I want it? Who can I influence and with what?

Communication is, on the one hand about what our intentions are when speaking and, on the other hand, about the words we use to express ourselves. One serious mistake, which really can complicate a dialogue, is when we focus on finding out who is to blame for what has happened. Another mistake is when we take our interpretations for truth. We believe we know the intentions of another even without asking. Here we get lost and attribute to the other person intentions that may not be correct. This can create a wall that will stand in the way of connection. A curious attitude is usually what is needed, as well as an openness to learn something new. To allow oneself to be surprised! This is not always easy, but it is possible.

Conflicts are often about a moral dilemma. It becomes more difficult to manage a conflict if we get stuck in a "right or wrong" way of thinking. Working with the office door open is not more "right" than to have it closed. But if we think or say that the person who wants it closed is "a coward" or that he or she "should be more open," the conflict becomes more difficult to manage. It is easier when we listen for the needs of the people involved and then search for a strategy that will meet those needs.

Dealing with a "right or wrong quarrel"

First of all. Stop focusing on trying to find out who is right or who is wrong! When you notice that someone is focused on finding a scapegoat, or on whose "fault" something is, switch your focus to one of the following things:

1. Say what you feel right now and what you long for, need and want. Ask what the other person feels, needs and wants. Help others to find ways to express this and ask yourself for help to do the same if you need it.

2. If you do not manage to connect, return to the topic that started the quarrel. Check if you have mixed in one or more interpretations with the observations you made of what happened.

3. If you do not manage to connect, propose a break. Use the break to get clear about what you feel, need and want. You can also ask a third person for help in sorting out what you really want to say or do.

4. Ask for help. Ask someone to help you focus on what needs to be said, listened to or done, instead of continuing to look for who is wrong or did something wrong.

To communicate with needs as a kind of anchor, helps you understand that someone who wants to have the door closed might have a need for peace and silence to be able to focus. The person who wants it open might have a need for connection and trust. Once you have put "all the cards on the table", look for solutions that are not based on right or wrong, but on how these needs can be met. One strategy in this case could be that the door is open at certain times of the day when the person who wants it closed is doing things that do not require so much concentration. If that does not work, another solution could be to schedule joint coffee breaks or other solutions that also include the needs for connection and trust.

In order to shift focus away from "right and wrong" thinking, focus on the answers to the following four questions:

1. What has happened? (Observations, facts) What have you seen or heard?

2. What do I/you feel in relation to what has happened? (Feelings)

3. What do I/you need? What am I/are you interested in and what do I/you long for? (Needs, values, hopes, dreams.)

4. What do I/you want to happen in order to meet as many needs as possible? (Requests, strategies)

1. Observation – Facts.

What have your senses really picked up and what have you added to with your thoughts about it?

If we want to communicate to solve any misunderstanding, it is valuable to be able to answer the question: "What has (really) happened?"

The question may seem easy to answer but it often becomes unnecessarily difficult. Being able to see what has happened and not mix it with interpretations, labels or judgments is a major challenge in all communication. First and foremost, we need to learn to see the difference between what has happened and our judgments about it, whether we judged it as bad, good, appropriate, inappropriate, wrong or fair. Thoughts of who did right and who did wrong cloud our view.

To create a connection that works, we need to discover what we think, transform the interpretations we are making, and try to see the situation from both our and the other person's points of view. What is described in terms of what we have seen and heard will likely lead to connection? There is a big difference between hearing someone describe facts about what they have seen and to hear their interpretations of what they have seen. "When I saw you walking out of the meeting room yesterday..." in contrast to "When I see how you ignore the rest of us and just turn away..." While the second sentence easily will be perceived as criticism, the first one has the potential to get the other person to stop and reflect. (Of course this is just the beginning of the conversation. The other questions in the box on the previous page usually also need to be answered.)

The specific observations I choose to communicate also show what is important to me. Some things that may seem really big may go unnoticed, whereas something that seems really trivial might evoke strong reactions.

In a working group I was part of, there was a conflict that got really difficult to sort out and we could not find "common ground". One person said that he had done what he had been asked to undertake and even claimed that he had done more than what was agreed on. The rest of us did not see how he could understand the situation in that way, because the commitment he had undertaken was far from complete in our eyes. After a while I decided to try to really understand and let go of my own right and wrong thinking. The more I listened, the clearer our "separate worlds" became. What he meant when he said he had done more than was agreed upon, was that he had done other things in hopes of reaching the goal, without asking us. He equated these things with what he had been asked to do, and according to his definition, he had thus done more than he had agreed to. As long as I heard him argue that he had done more, at the same time as we sat there with the idea that the task had actually not been finished, all my focus had been on proving him wrong. When I got his view of the situation, it became easier to drop my arguments for why he was wrong and we were right and focus on finding a solution for the present situation.

Focusing on who is to blame for something or trying to find out who has done something wrong, rarely leads us to a good connection. But listening and clearly expressing our own observations might.

One of the reasons why we might find it difficult to stick to facts and instead express ourselves with judgments and evaluations are that we might feel pain in relation to what has happened. When we do not express what we feel, judgments become a way, albeit vague, of asking for understanding for the pain we are experiencing.

Therefore, the second question to answer in communication where we seek connection is:

"What do I and others feel in relation to what has happened."

2. What do you feel?

REFLECTION:
What is your relationship to emotions? Is it easy or not for you to put words to your feelings?
How it is for you when others express their feelings? Are some emotions more uncomfortable than others?
Do you believe the way you communicate your emotions affects your communication with others?
In what way?

Difficult conversations not only concern strong feelings, they are all about feelings. Sometimes someone says that one should "stick to the facts" in a conflict. But if the connection is disturbed and feelings are strong, we usually need to address the emotional part of the conflict before we get to the facts. Sometimes we try to hide what we feel and believe that others will not notice anything. But when we do not express what we feel, and simultaneously feel strong emotions, others usually pay attention to exactly that. Just think about how you react when someone seems angry, nervous, scared or anxious but does not express it. We notice that something is going on and the less we hear about it, the more attention it will attract. When someone who is feeling strong emotions is willing to openly name that fact, others have clarity and so they can automatically focus on what the aim of the meeting is (rather than on trying to understand what is going on with someone). The others are no longer wondering about what the person is concealing, or when she or he will explode, and are instead able to put their focus onto a task, or onto sorting out what is most valuable for everyone involved.

REFLECTION:
How do you react when someone expresses what she or he feels? Would you prefer that she or he would not express it, or do you appreciate that people put words to their feelings? Are there some feelings you would rather not hear about?

It is valuable to develop your emotional vocabulary. Listed below are suggestions of words for feelings that describe what is happening within us and that is not so easily perceived as criticism of others.

Afraid	Desperate	Hoppful	Skeptical
Alive	Disappointed	Impatient	Stressed
Ambivalent	Disinterested	Irritated	Sure
Angry	Downhearted	Lonely	Surprised
Ashamed	Embarrassed	Moved	Suspicious
Awake	Energetic	Nervous	Tense
Bored	Enthusiastic	Overwhelmed	Thrilled
Calm	Frustrated	Perplexed	Tired
Comfortable	Furious	Proud	Uncomfortable
Confused	Gloomy	Restless	Uneasy
Curious	Grateful	Sad	Upset
Delighted	Grumpy	Satisfied	Vulnerable
Depressed	Happy	Shocked	Worried

To develop a vocabulary of emotions according to the list on the previous page is useful for several reasons. When we use words to express what is happening in us that mix what we feel with what we think, it is usually more difficult for others to listen to us with care and interest.

If I say:
"I feel manipulated,"

it is much easier for others to hear that as criticism than if I say:
"I feel worried."

In the first case, we have woven together what we think other people's intentions are with what we feel. It tends to lead to more resistance than willingness to listen.

Here is a list of words commonly used to describe emotions, but where the feeling is mixed with a thought, usually with a thought about what others have done:

Abandoned	Controlled	Intimidated	Reduced
Absorbed	Deceived	Manipulated	Subdued
Abused	Fooled	Mistrusted	Threatened
Attacked	Forced	Misunderstood	Violated
Betrayed	Harassment	Neglected	
Bullied	Ignored	Neglected	

A person who attended one of my trainings was working as an administrator at a state institution. When we discussed what kind of space emotions could have in a professional attitude, her reaction was this:

"Some feelings would not be ok for me to express in my professional role. Though I value honesty, I could not imagine, for example, saying "I feel sad because I need respect" or "I feel annoyed because I yearn for support on this issue."

We talked further about the intention beyond expressing feelings. At the end of the training this person told me with satisfaction in her voice that she had found a way to be honest and open, without using words she experienced as charged or uncomfortable.

REFLECTION:
Are there situations when you are not willing to express what is going on inside you in words? Are you clear about how it affects your environment?

It is important to remember that it is not an end in itself to use certain words. What is important is that the other person can understand you, and that you create connection. It not necessary to state that you feel "sad" if you think that is not appropriate in a workplace or other kind of formal setting. It can help the connection if you clarify that there is "a lot going on" or some other statement that fits. In some situation it can be easier for others to hear the word "insecure" rather than "afraid" or "frustrated" rather than "angry".

REFLECTION:
How do you react when someone who seems to feel strong emotions is not willing to tell you what is going on within him or her?

Everything doesn't becomes "fine and dandy" just because people express what they feel. Some people even argue the opposite. Many people has experienced situations where emotions were expressed in a way that led to guilt or shame. It might be challenging to listen to what someone else feels if we hear it as if we are the reason they feel that way.

The most effective way I have found to create connection when expressing emotions, which does not lead to guilt and shame, is to connect what I or the other person feels to what I or the other person values. In this way, emotions seem to be more okay; they are perceived as relevant and are thus less questioned. Feelings are neither amplified nor diminished when they are taken into account as a way to identify the needs and values that each person is seeking.

People can recognize and accept that someone feels lonely when they long for community, sad when they need support or bored when they want to experience meaning.

When we stop blaming our feelings on others, we get more power to handle the situation. We can now focus on that which we have the power to influence – what is going on inside us – and less about what we do not have power over – what others want and do.

Express:
"I feel sad because I long for more community."
"I am worried because I'm longing for connection."
"I feel annoyed because I wanted to get the project application ready today in order to take one step closer to the goal."

Rather than:
"I feel sad because YOU do not want to be with me."
"I feel worried because YOU do not talk to me."
"I feel annoyed because YOU do not support me."

REFLECTION:
How do you react when someone makes you responsible for what they feel?
In what situations do you blame others for what you feel?
What are the needs that come alive here?
How would you like to react?

Next, the third question, which is valuable in all human communication:
What do you and I need?

Some other ways to ask the same question:
What are you interested in?

What would you like to happen?
What do you long for?
What do you dream of?

3. Needs, Interests, Dreams, Values, Longings - What do you need?

We can choose to blame our feelings on what that someone else has done or not done. Or we can trace our feelings to our childhood, link them to stress, chemicals and so on. I suggest that you use your feelings to connect to your needs. One of the values of connecting what we feel to our needs is that others don't as easily hear our feelings as criticism of them. This will make it easier to connect.

Instead of saying:

"I feel sad because you do not support me"
"I feel upset because you demand so much of me",

we can say:

"I feel sorry because I long so much for community in this, would you like to tell me more of what makes you say no to what I'm asking for?",

or:

"I feel upset because I want to be seen as truly doing everything I can to be of help."

When I use the word need, I mean something all humans share. Needs are motivating forces that everyone can recognize in whatever position or role they may have. Whether we see ourselves as a customer, guest, employee, director, officer, receptionist or travel guide, we will all be able to recognize ourselves in words such as: respect, freedom, community, love, care, empowerment, acceptance, to be seen and heard, meaning, stimulation, rest, intimacy, food, water and sleep.

As we recognize ourselves in others, we can also understand why something may be important to someone else. Sometimes the word "need" might feel difficult to use, and then words like "what we value, want, long for or dream of", might fit better.

Some Basic Human Needs

Connection
acceptance
appreciation
belonging
cooperation
communication
closeness
community
companionship
compassion
consideration
consistency
empathy
inclusion
intimacy
love
mutuality
nurturing
respect/self-respect
safety
security
stability
support
to know and be known
to see and be seen
to understand and be understood
trust
warmth

Physical well-being
air/food
movement/exercise
rest/sleep
sexual expression
safety
shelter
touch
water

Honesty
authenticity
integrity
presence

Play
joy
humor

Peace
beauty
communion
ease
equality
harmony
inspiration
order

Autonomy
choice
freedom
independence
space
spontaneity

Meaning
awareness
celebration of life
challenge
clarity
competence
consciousness
contribution
creativity
discovery
efficacy
effectiveness
growth
hope
learning
mourning
participation
purpose
self-expression
stimulation
to matter
understanding

4. Positive Request - What strategies would help you meet your needs?

There is a fourth important question to answer when our purpose is to connect:
"What can I or others ask for that could meet our needs?"

To express what we feel and need seems to motivate people to act. But they do not always act in ways that we would want them to, if we forget to add what we want them to do.

I have on occasion been invited to join different organizations' meetings in order to study the communication and identify the reasons that, for example, misunderstandings occur so often. They may regularly have customers that complain about something even though what they do or sell is working and want to understand why this keeps happening.

After meetings like that, I often felt confused and wondered what actually had been agreed upon. When asking those participating, it indeed turned out that there were many different opinions about what was actually decided. It was not really strange that when a customer received these different messages they ended up not knowing what to trust.

"Repeat!"

Many of us have realized that it is useful to assume that people, including ourselves, often misunderstand or distort information we receive from others. In some workgroups it is therefore worked into the work routine to ask co-workers to repeat information. Air traffic controllers, surgeons and soldiers know that a misunderstanding may endanger the lives of others. Therefore, they use this effective tool to ensure safety.

Since relationships are essential to our well being, it is of great importance that our communication is working as well, even when it is not a life-threatening situation. Asking someone to repeat what they have heard can help protect relationships that are important to us.

Asking someone to "repeat" may not be so easy in some situations, for example, in a meeting with a customer.

Therefore, I want to give some suggestions on how we can ask others to reflect information:

"I'm not sure if I was clear and covered everything. Could you reflect back what you heard so I can see if there is something I need to add?"

"Could you with your own words tell me what you heard me say so I can see if I expressed myself clearly?"

"Would you be willing to tell me in your own words what you understood as important to me around this?"

"For me, this is a very important decision. I wonder if you could tell me how you perceived the decision, so I can know if we understood it in the same way? "

Some may feel resistance to the idea of asking someone to repeat what you have said. You may worry that others will think that you consider them stupid or that you are trying to patronize them. Since 1999, when I first started working with trainings on NVC, I have only twice heard someone react in a negative way when I asked him or her to repeat what she or he heard me say. Both times it helped me to be clearer about what my intention was in asking someone to reflect back what I had said.

You could say that there are two main categories of requests:
1. Requests with the purpose of establishing or strengthening the connection with the other person.
2. Requests with the purpose of getting something done.

If the purpose of our requests is primarily to protect the connection with the other person, it can be expressed in two different "directions". The first is to ask the other person to repeat what we have said. The second is to reflect back what we have heard the other person say, and then ask the other person to confirm if he or she has been perceived in the way he or she wanted.

Sometimes our requests may be perceived as demands or criticism, especially if they are repeated. John asks Matthew for the third time:

"I wonder if Nicholas received the information that we will not deal with the case until next month? Have you told him that?"

Matthew replies:
"Don't you think I am doing my job?"

Here it is obvious that Matthew is hearing something else than what John is asking for. He hears criticism or demands in what John is saying. It will probably be easier for Matthew not to hear John's question as criticism if John makes it clear why he is asking:

"I really care about keeping up the connection and trust with Nicholas's business and I am not sure I was fully clear about what I wanted us to do. I know I am repeating myself, but I wonder if you are willing to tell me if you have acted on this, or if there is anything else you would need in order to be able to do it?"

Here, John is taking on responsibility for not always being so clear, which may make it easier for Matthew to hear that John does not want to blame him for anything. If Matthew still experiences himself as being criticized, perhaps there is something that they need to talk about. Maybe John realizes that he actually has a concern that Matthew will not do his tasks because he has earlier missed something that was important. Maybe Matthew in his turn realizes that he is reading past "experiences" when he had been criticized into what John is now saying.

Another purpose of making requests is to try to understand what is important to the other person. If Matthew would answer no to the question, that he has not informed the customer, John can continue to ask questions such as:

"Could you say something more about how come he has not been informed?"

And if Matthew has said, *"Don't you think I am doing my job?"* *John can pick up that something seems to be going on that he is not aware of; "I guess what I just said brought something up in you. Are you willing to tell me what it's about?"*

Sometimes it is more important to express requests about getting something done, than to strengthen or deepen your connection. When we express a request for someone else to do something, it is important to be as clear as possible, but also that we express ourselves in ways that show we see there is a choice. Furthermore, we want to express our requests as specifically as possible in terms of time, place and person. We want to make sure that what we ask for is either doable in the present, or that someone is willing to say yes to do it at a later point.

These "action-focused" requests, for example, might sound like this:

"Are you willing to call Mary and ask her if she has informed Nicholas about the meeting?"

"Could you bring Nicholas's application with you when you come?"

"Are you willing to look through our policies and procedures for how we notify our customers in situations like this? Feel free to suggest a change if you see flaws that we can do something about."

"Could you go through the changes in procedures at the meeting tomorrow? "

When we have connection and a sense of flow in our communication, there is a margin for "negligence" in the way we communicate. But when the situation is tense or the relationship is very important, it is valuable to remember these guidelines and watch out for vague requests like:

"Someone should deal with this at once!"

"Don't you understand that such a low level of service is unacceptable!"

"This place is a mess!"

Another thing to remember when it comes to requests is that we will probably be most satisfied with the results if we ask for what we want instead of asking for what we do not want. If we express what we do not want, the other person might stop doing what we ask for, but at the same time it might be that he or she will do something even more destructive instead.

To get the maximum effect of your requests, make sure they are:
- Clear (in terms of person, time, place, action).
- Positive; possible to respond to, or act on, in the present moment.
- Doable.

When Requests Turn into Demands

If it is not clear to us that our needs may be met in many different ways, we may think that we have to force someone to do exactly what we want. To demand or to express what we want and threaten with some kind of punishment if it does not happen is likely to reduce others' willingness to help us. Therefore, if someone says no to our request, we want to keep communicating until both parties are satisfied.[1]

When we hear demands we do one of two things. Either we rebel, which creates resistance and callousness. Or we submit, we give up and agree to things we do not like - which also creates distance. There will be less caring and willingness to help each other if this happens.

When a person in a position of authority expresses a request, it can easily be perceived as a demand, no matter how it is expressed. When our boss, our father, our mother, our priest, our doctor or our teacher says something, we quite easily might find ourselves

---

1 More about that in Chapter 5 – To Say No and still keep connection on page 166

doing something against our will, which affects the relationship in the long run. This is especially relevant if a history of threats, demands and different kinds of punishment have been involved in the relationship. Some people end up in rebellion and will not do what a person in authority asks for, just because he or she is a person of authority.

If we want cooperation that is based on anything other than coercion and feelings of duty, we can watch out for words like should, must, have to and so on. But now you may be thinking – yeah, but sometimes I actually want to demand something, what can I do? "Sometimes things just have to be done!" Maybe you are a project manager or a director of a project that has a deadline on Thursday and you realize that several steps are missing before it will be ready. Then, of course, it is tempting to say:

"You HAVE TO be finished with this at the latest on Thursday at 10 o'clock!"

Sure you can say this, but if the other person hears it as a de-mand, there is a risk that he or she will either rebel or just do as you say whether they like it or not. But their trust in your care about their wellbeing may decrease. If you want things done and at the same time cherish cooperation, you can say something like this instead:

"When I see that X is not finished yet, I get a bit stressed. I'm con-cerned that it will not be ready on Thursday either. I really want to show this customer that they can trust that we will deliver when we said we would. So I wonder, what do you need for it to be ready at the latest on Thursday at 10 o'clock?"

If you want to move fast, go alone.
If you want to go far, go together.
Proverb from Ghana[2]

---

[2] "If you want to go fast, go alone. If you want to go far, go together." From www.nonviolentcommunica-tion.com januari 2011.

People easily hear what we say as criticism:

1. If we only tell them what we think and feel.

2. If we only tell them what we feel.

3. When we mix what we feel with interpretations of other people's purposes with something they do.

4. If we express requests or demands without giving an explanation of how we hope it will contribute to everyone involved.

5. If our request isn't clear for the other person. They might then easily hear it as if they "should" understand what to do and as criticism of the fact that they have not already done so.

People do not as easily hear criticism if we:

1. Only tell what we have seen them do or heard them say (without analyzing if what they did was good, right, bad, normal or appropriate).

2. Follow up on what we feel and take responsibility for it by telling what needs of ours are the reason for these feelings.

3. When we, after taking the steps described in one and two, follow up with what we want them to do with the information. That is, what we would like to hear from them or what we would like them to do.

Body Language

I think we are born with the ability to interpret body language. Or at least with the some ability to pick up information about the emotional states of people close to us. We perceive when someone is angry or sad without them saying anything about it. It is a kind of survival instinct that has stayed with us to varying degrees.

The most important thing when it comes to body language is to take in what we see, while not taking for granted that we know what is going on in someone else.

I remember how relieved I felt some years ago when I read the newspaper headline "Body language lies." The article described how we, through books and seminars, have been led to believe that a certain gesture or posture always means the same thing, though they are expressed by different people and in different situations. Over the past three decades I was often worried about how I heard people talk about their ability to read body language and to describe it very mechanically. Those who lectured or wrote about body language probably had the intention of facilitating cooperation and communication between people. And perhaps in their eagerness to contribute, they may have simplified their message too much, making it possible to use their ideas as a weapon, because at times I have heard people judge others based on their ideas about body language. I am interested in perceiving signals about what people feel and need, even when they cannot express it with words. I am not interested in interpreting body language according to some general templates. I am interested in getting my own body language and the words I use to match each other, so that others do not have to doubt what is going on within me.

If I am to read other people's body signals, I want to do it with an approach that is likely to awaken my compassion and willingness to contribute to them. When we feel irritated or stressed, the people around us often perceive it. If they hear that we are aware of how we feel, it is easier for them to deal with our irritation, at least if we do not blame them. When we feel anxious or fearful, it may sometimes appear as if we are hostile or angry. Then it is a gift to hear that we are so busy trying to deal with what is going on inside us, that we simply are not focused on connecting with others.

When Self-image is Threatened, Connection is Threatened

EXAMPLE 1

He stated that I was trying to stop him and ruin his career. Saying said things like, "I've done everything that everyone else has done and more, and yet I did not get the job."

My view was different and I was angry that he omitted important fact about himself and me when he talked with others. I got really frustrated as I realized that others believed his distorted view of the situation. Inside me I longed for get back at her, my self-image was threatened and I had to force myself to keep listening to her.

EXAMPLE 2

When a woman asked a man why he did not contact her, he replied that he felt cool toward her because the memory of her slapping him was still strong. He stated that even though the slap happened 10 years earlier he could still feel it. The woman denied it and called him sick and crazy. She exclaimed that she was not a person who uses violence! The connection became even more difficult because her self-image was threatened.

If communication between two people threatens either of their self-image, this may get in the way of their connection. Therefore, it is important to find a way to be fully honest and at the same time recognize that the conversation may be a big challenge for the other person. Fortunately, there are concrete things we can do in these situations. One is to sort out what is fact and what is an interpretation of what has happened. This cannot be repeated enough. With facts, I mean things we have seen or heard or otherwise taken in with our senses (and that others also may have seen or heard). Think of the difference between what a movie camera has actually filmed as opposed to the review of that movie. When we talk about what happened (facts), rather than our interpretations, it is easier for others to listen to us.

If we feel that our self-image is threatened, we can do the same thing and distinguish between my actual observable actions and other people's or my own interpretations of them.

REFLECTION:

What could threaten my self-image during a difficult conversation?

Does the ground shake under my feet if someone calls me mean, selfish or arrogant.

Or would the worst thing be if someone claimed that I do not want to contribute or help? That I'm self-centered!

What would happen to me (my view of who I am and what I am worth) if, for example, I got a "no" in a salary negotiation?

How do I want to come across during and after a difficult conversation where my self-image was questioned?

Take No Shit!

In a swedish TV show called "Grynets Show", Elin Ek's "alter ego" coined the expression "take no crap". I agree with her, and suggest that when we hear what someone says to us as if he or she is "throwing crap" at us, we try to stop listening to the other person's judgments of us, and instead listen to what she or he needs. If we hear someone criticizing us, it is a sign that we do not hear his or her needs, and it will complicate our connection. Think about when you hear criticism. Someone is saying that you failed or that you did a bad job. There are other ways to handle this than to agree and judge ourselves, or to fight back and claim the opposite. A third way when we experience being criticized is to try to "see the human being" in ourselves or others by:

1. Trying to see the other person as a human being. That is, connecting to what the person is feeling and needing in that moment.

2. Reminding yourself that you are "only human". That is, getting in touch with what you are feeling and needing in this moment.

3. Start from these two points of views when you start talking.

Guest: This was terrible! Such idiots, is your service always this bad?

If you forget to focus on connection you might make the situation worse by answering:
We are the best in town, but you gave us such short notice!

If instead you want to try a more connecting comment, it might sound like this: I hear that you are really dissatisfied and disappointed that the result was not at all like what you had hoped for?!

Guest: *Well this just does not work.*

Connection answer: *You're worried because this part really needs to work to get your project ahead?*

Guest: *Yes exactly.*

Connection answer: *I would like to tell you how this is for me and then see what we can do to set this OK for you?*

Guest: *Sure, go ahead.*

Connection answer:
I am also keen to make this work. At the same time I notice that it was a little difficult to listen to the way you expressed it. I would like to help and at the same time I want to experience respect in the conversation between us, how is it for you to hear this?
Guest: *Yes ... I was pretty upset.*

Connection answer:
Yes, I can understand that, you've got a lot invested in this. At the same time for the future I would like to ask you that, when you are upset, you would say what you want instead of calling us names, what do you need in order to do that?

Guest: : *I'm not sure.*

Connection answer: So maybe we need to talk about this at another time. Lets see what can we do now, when things are this crazy?!

We need to evaluate on a case-by-case basis if we would rather directly address the "problem" and only then bring up how the person's tone and words affected us.

Honesty

"If you do not stand up for something you will fall for anything."

Generally, one can say that a relationship is strengthened by honesty and honesty contributes to trust. This is of course the case when it comes to not withholding the truth or distorting it. But it also matters what it is that I am honest about. I have often heard the question: "But how can I be honest? You can not tell everything?! At least not in this workplace!"

An approach that helps me is to not see honesty as an end in itself. We can see honesty as a means to get connection. To express what I am nervous of telling is a way to make myself human.

Sometimes I hear people deliver "truths" to people and argue that they do this because it is so important to be straight forward. What we call "our truth", though, is often properly mixed with interpretations and analyzes of the other person and his or her intention. For me, there is nothing "straight forward" in telling me that someone, for example, is lazy, stupid or selfish. These are interpretations and expressing them rarely leads to connection. What you are honest with is important to choose if you want to maximize the odds to create connection and facilitate cooperation.

Express:

· What you see and hear.

· What you feel.

· What you need and want.

· Requests you might have.

Do not express:

· Judgments of the other person - that is, personal attacks like "you are lazy, stupid or selfish".

· What you think she or he has done wrong, at least not in the initial stages before you have established connection.

· What she or he should or must do, especially not before you are connected.

Be honest in situations:

· That bother you and where enemy images or escalating conflict may easily arise.

· That can hurt you, others, or material things.

· Where yours or other people's needs are not being met.

· Where the same information is presented differently depending on whether the meeting is informal or formal.

If we do not think that the other person is opening up to see their part in the conflict, we can choose to be open about what we feel and want ourselves. It may help the other person to lower her or his guard and open up. She or he can no longer hide behind excuses like: "If she does not intend to be honest, then I'm not going to expose myself."

Expressing feelings make us human and therefore more secure to open up to. Honesty about how something affects us can make others embarrassed, but it can help them "save their face" in similar situations in the future. The story below has taught me not to judge other people's dishonesty so hard.

During a period in my life I noticed that I sometimes lied to a man I had a close relationship with. It was not about "big things", but it was almost like an automatic reaction when he asked me about something. For example, if I had forgotten to turn the light off in the kitchen and he asked me if I had. One day I heard myself assuring him that I had plugged in the car heating cable, which I had not done, I realized that I said it in an attempt to avoid criticism. We had built up a communication pattern where we both criticized each other. It had resulted in a slight discomfort that I constantly was mentally prepared for and wanted to protect myself against. When I brought it up with him, it turned out that he recognized the discomfort and the tendency to try to get away from it.

It was a turning point when both he and I realized that I was vulnerable in these situations and that I was not lying in order to deceive him but to protect me from being questioned. It has helped me to not judge people who find it difficult to speak the truth. Perhaps they are in the same vulnerable position as I was in and do not feel confident enough that they will be responded to in a caring way if they do tell the truth. I do not mean that I just want to accept that someone chooses not to tell the truth, but I have learned that there can be many reasons behind the choice to lie, of which I have no idea.

Humour

To have fun when you meet the people you see as guests or customers may make both you and them feel good. At the same time, there are things to be mindful about when it comes to using humor.

Humor can both unite and contribute to divisions within groups. When first meeting people, be careful about how and what you joke about. While sarcasm or irony might help lighten the mood of a conversation, they can also create a lot of tension.

If we have a position of power, such as a manager, it is even more sensitive to choose the type of jokes we use. Often people laugh at the boss's jokes, even when they feel uneasy and M if the joke contains some innuendo or covert criticism.

With new acquaintances, a similar effect can occur and it will often not come up until you have gotten to know each other a little more. There can be laughter, yet it may leave a bitter taste in the mouth.

No matter what position you have, or whom you have contact with, I suggest you think about why you use humor, what your intention is. If you realize that you want to meet some other needs than to have fun together when joking, you might want to consider whether to do it or not. I suggest that you refrain entirely from making jokes if you notice that you use jokes to lighten up feedback you are afraid to receive. The same applies if you use jokes to criticize, disarm or punish someone. If there is something you want to bring up, but are not sure how you will be received, perhaps you can ask for help from someone else in communicating. Even if your intention is to have fun and "lighten the mood", others still may perceive it as if you are teasing them, or making fun at their expense.

In "Provocative coaching" there are some ideas on how to consciously use humor to support others to be clear about what they need and want. One of the approaches in provocative coaching;

"don't´ be an expert, be a fool," is especially helpful in my opinion. This approach helps me focus on connecting with others rather than defending my truth. Many times, a willingness to drop all the ideas I have about me knowing something, has helped me to keep my curiosity and thus be able to stay more open to other world views.

> REFLECTION:
> *Are you aware of why you are joking, what your purpose is?*
> *Can you change your way of joking if you notice that you do it in a way that others hear as criticism or it makes them insecure?*
> *Is there warmth in your jokes?*

To handle conflicts

"He drew a circle to keep me out,
A thing of scorn, and a thing to flout.
But love and I had the wit to win:
We drew a circle that took him in."
EDWIN MARKHAM[3]

In a conflict, it is easy to draw conclusions that give us the greatest benefits. We think that we are better than others, that they do not deserve our respect because of their behavior. If we want to create connection, we can ask: What does she see that I do not? What needs does he understand are at risk that I do not perceive?

The approach that has served me the most is to assume that behind everything that people do, there is an intention to meet needs. It has helped me time and time again to drop any ideas about who did right and who did wrong, and instead focus on the needs we tried to meet doing what we did. I do not claim that needs are the only thing that motivates people to act. But I say that if we focus on the needs behind someone's behavior, it is easier for us to see the person behind the conflict and connect

---

[3] http://en.wikiquote.org/wiki/Edwin_Markham. 27 dec 2010.

with them.

When in conflict, I sometimes find that my way of thinking magnifies what I feel in a way that makes it more difficult to communicate. When I am in pain my thoughts keep me from being open-minded. I become narrow in my thinking, certain I know the motivation of others. This certainty interferes with curiosity and connection. There may be thoughts like: I know exactly what he meant. I can see what kind of a person she is. While I may not share my thoughts out loud, this inner stance keeps me from listening deeply to the other and hinders my willingness to communicate. Another way to deal with a challenging situation is to distinguish between what we believe is the intent of someone's actions and the outcome of it. Even though the choices of another person were uncomfortable or painful for us, it does not mean that the person's intention was to cause us pain. A clue to distinguish between these two things is to first detect our interpretations and then to go back to the observation. We can ask ourselves:
What do I think about the other person and her or his intentions?
(That is, what is our interpretation)

And then distinguish the answer from the answer to the questions below:
What did I actually hear the other person say? What did I see him do?
(That is, what we have observed)
Then focus on the emotions of this moment:
How was I affected by what I saw or heard? What did I feel in that situation?

Once we have answered these questions, it may be clear how it happened that we made the assumption we did about the other person's intention. Remember that I am not asking you to do this to minimize or take away what you feel. I ask you to do it to find what stimulated your emotion and what was the real reason for it. Just because we feel disappointed it does not mean that the other person's intention was to let us down. Just because we feel insecure it does not mean that the person had the intention to make us insecure.

Once we have separated between what actually happened from what we think about it, we can communicate to the other person how his or her behavior affected us.

Now you may be wondering if it really is a wise idea to actually say what you thought the other person's intentions were. If you plan to do so, be prepared for the other person to start defending him or herself. Most people do not appreciate having their intentions judged by others, especially if it involves intentionally hurting others. People want to be seen for doing the best they can no matter how challenging the situation is for them.

When we feel hurt, it is easy to believe that the other person's intention was to hurt us. If we feel misunderstood, it is easy to think that the other person does not bother to try to understand. But what we feel and what the other person's intention was, is not nearly as close as they seem. We all live and act from our own universe with the information we currently have.

Misunderstandings about the intentions of other people jeopardize our relationship with them. We accuse others of having bad intentions. This usually makes others want to argue to prove that they indeed did not have any bad intentions. This, in turn, leads to us not feeling understood. Our opinion about them becomes true and our enemy images of each other only become stronger.

On the other hand if we are accused of having bad intentions, it usually does not help to try and explain what our intentions were. Our explanations does not ease the pain of the other person, at least not before they have been heard in what it is that hurts them. Therefore, first listen to the person's feelings and needs, and only then tell him or her what your purpose was for doing what you did. Talk about what needs motivated you to act as you did, whether you are now proud of the result or not.

REFLECTION:
When things go wrong, some of us often tend to blame ourselves while others tend to blame someone else when things go wrong. If you are clear about which of these positions you usually act from, you can get clues to new ways to manage conflicts that reoccur in your surrounding. Be honest with yourself. If you usually finding yourself blaming others, try taking time to reflect upon what part you have contributed to the conflict. If you usually find yourself thinking you are totally responsible for any conflict, ask yourself what you could ask from the other person to create a solution to the problem at hand.

Listen Yourself Out Of The Conflict

The most effective tool to downsize a conflict is to listen. By listening I mean not to just be quiet. I mean to listen in a way that makes it clear to the other person that we are interested in understanding his or her point of view. It is about listening for the "right things", ie the essence of what the other person wants us to hear and to be able to reflect back that we really have listened.

We want to be able to listen to others, but without taking what they say personally and giving in on things that are important to us. Linking what another person feels to what she or he needs, usually makes it easier to avoid taking what is said personally.

When it is Time To Invite a Mediator

Many times it is valuable to use the support of a third party on occasions when important values or human well-being is threatened by a conflict[4]. Unfortunately, we often wait too long because it

---

[5] If you want to read more about mediation, you can read my book A Helping Hand, Mediation with Nonviolent Communication. Friare Liv.

may feel embarrassing to show others that we are in a conflict and that we need support. Ask yourself if you really have something to lose by asking for the support of any independent party.

Think of mediation as a conversation which a third party is trying to make easier. Mediation helps the participants understand the needs behind what is being said. This includes the skill of translating difficult messages such as labels, demands or threats into needs. A mediator also helps the participants show that they have heard the other. And then supports them in building an agreement for the future that is clear and doable for all.

Real Apologizing includes Listening

A common question in our trainings is about how to "rewind" a bad dialogue and turn around dialogues that have gotten out of hand. Far too many people have unresolved conflicts that have been draining energy for a long time because they cannot find a way back into connection with a person who is important to them. To simply apologize is one way to "rewind" a dialogue. It can sometimes be enough to be able to start with "a clean slate".

Unfortunately, an "I apologize or "I'm sorry, it was my fault" can be heard as a way to try to smooth things over without each person being heard or taking responsibility for their part. It is actually not very satisfying in many situations. If it is perceived in this way, we can try to show that we are willing to consider how our choices have affected the other person and that we are willing to look for ways to repair the trust between us.

The next time you apologize to someone, I suggest that you begin by trying to understand what she or he feels. Have you ever thought about the fact that if you ask someone to forgive you, you are asking this person to do something for you? And this after you have done something that has been painful for him or her.

Therefore, I suggest that you first ask if the other person has something more they want to say about the situation and that only after listening do you ask someone to forgive you. When we have listened to other people, they usually like to hear why we acted as we did. Now we can tell them which of our needs we tried to meet and what intention we had in acting in this way. People are rarely interested in excuses or even explanations. But they are usually genuinely interested in what was going on inside of us in that moment. In this situation it is important to listen to the other person's pain if it is stimulated again.

Apologizing

Step 1. Listen and find out how your actions have influenced the other person.

Step 2. Once you have taken in what is said, tell the other person what happens in you when you understand how your actions affected him or her.

Step 3. Tell the other person which needs you were trying to meet by choosing to do what you did. Express what it was that motivated you, even if you after realizing the consequences would choose another way to act. Be prepared at any time to go back to step 1.

Communicate with "difficult people"

"One wants to be loved, in lack thereof admired, in lack thereof feared, in lack thereof loathed and despised. One wants to instill some sort of emotion in people. The soul trembles before emptiness and desires contact at any price." (From Doctor Glas)

HJALMAR SÖDERBERG

Hjalmar Söderberg wrote these words in his novel Doctor Glas as early as 1905. They have often helped me to remember that we all have a need to be seen and taken into consideration.

The foundation of all human connection is that we see each other and help each other fill that "gap" between us. We can never completely control an encounter with another human being. But we can prepare for encounters, we can train ourselves to connect with people, we can practice the things we think are challenging or are recurrently difficult for us. The truth is that there are no "difficult people", but there are situations that we experience as awkward because we do not know how to reach out to one another.

An important part in handling these difficult situations is to think about what this person mirrors to us about ourselves. Imagine that you have just set the labels "demanding" or "unintelligent" on a guest, customer or client. Many of us blame ourselves after judging others. We judge ourselves for being "terrible" or "selfish" to have these thoughts. Interacting with this person interferes with our self-image of being a caring and warm person. It can lead us to say yes to things in order to protect our self-image or simply to get rid of the other person. It may mean that we agree to things we later regret. When we are prepared to see that we, like everyone else, sometimes get stuck in judgments, we can be clear about where and when we want to say yes and no.

REFLECTION:
In what situations is your self-image questioned?

When do you act in a way that makes you think "I can't believe I'm thinking/acting/saying this."

When do you receive criticism that pulls you out of balance?

What positive judgments about yourself are in danger and/or do you want to defend in a way that does not benefit you and the others around you?

If you want to go deeper, do the exercise on Preparing to Meet a Difficult Person on page 158.

Chapter 4

How we treat the customer reflects how well we function internally as a group

REFLECTION:
How would we (as a business or workplace) like to be perceived by those who connect with us?

What can we do to influence things so they evolve in that direction?

What do we need to do to make it possible for us to take steps in that direction?

The Receptionist - The Display Window of a Team

An official who participated in one of our trainings could not understand what his coworkers were talking about when they discussed a group of bothersome customers. When he told the others about this, the receptionist glared at him, but said nothing (maybe because he was her boss). But when he commented on this for the third time, she could no longer hold her tongue any longer and blurted out:

"Yes, but then you don't know that we have met them five times before we let them in to see you. So we have already been listening to their complaints, giving them information, asking them to come back and putting up with a thing or two that they would probably never say to you."

Situations like the one above often come up in trainings I do in workplaces. When an organization is criticized for the way

79

they treat their clients or customers, it easily happens that the blame falls on the receptionist or others who have had the first direct contact with them. Certainly, those who first meet the upset guests, might need additional training and support. At the same time it's also valuable to focus on how the rest of the organization is functioning and how clear the organization's goals are.

Imagine that you have just started working in a restaurant and you have been clearly requested to always be courteous to your customers at all times. The owner claims, "the customer is always right", and says that you should always give the customers what they want. You have just received the third order for vegetarian food today, even though there are no vegetarian dishes on the menu.

The two previous times when you gave the chef the order, she sighed loudly, stared at you and said, "Can you stop being so troublesome. Just tell them to order from the menu we have". The third customer asking for vegetarian food will certainly not receive your best smile. You are so tense about turning this order over to the chef that you just frown and gives a short answer.

If you are the guest at this restaurant and are longing for some good vegetarian food, it is easy to blame the waitress for poor service. You might call her unfriendly or cold. But if we could only talk to her, perhaps she would blame the chef and we might do the same. A third possibility is to argue that it is the owner who has made such unreasonable demands and that it is not always possible to say yes to everything. Regardless of how we see this, it is clear that anyone finding themselves in stressful daily conflicts with the working group they are part of, while at the same time expected to respond positively to the customers, is truly challenged to be accommodating at all times.

For the waitress to feel angry and crave respect in one moment, and then to smile and look as if nothing has happened in the next, it is not only difficult, but can also be perceived as suspicious and even phony to the customer. To feel insecure and in the next moment to have to contribute to making a customer feel comfortable is a big challenge. Few of us can go from one emotional state to another in such a short time as is sometimes required of us in a work situation. Generally, one could say that an encounter with a customer will work out only as well as the teamwork of the organization works. If your organization are criticized for not responding to customers in a good way, it is valuable both to learn how to do so, but also to devote time and energy to thinking about how the teamwork in your organization is functioning. A team that focuses on cooperation rather than on competition, on continuous supportive feedback, rather than on silence or talking behind each other's backs, is more likely to get more positive feedback from the outside. Now I hope no one hears this as a criticism if you are not getting the appreciation you want, but as a possible clue as to where you can start working to improve your work situation.

The Well-being of The Group Affects Connections With the Individual

Connecting to people is first and foremost about meeting needs. For example, in an airplane there is great emphasis on safety and therefore it is important that conflicts or strong emotions do not arise during a flight. Therefore the personnel keep to a strict, polite but friendly tone, when addressing the passengers and when giving information. Who does what and the order of all procedures are carefully planned in advance.

Many airlines break up the teams of flight attendants so that they do not work with each other over a long period of time. Therefore the teams rarely achieve more than the first phase of group development, which is very effective in that particular situation. Confined up in the air, in a narrow space, people are grateful not to have to listen to staff conflicts, which might arise were the teams to spend more time together.

In most work groups it is useful for the group to receive support in helping the group to mature, to manage conflicts, talking about challenges and how the group wants the leadership to work.

Only when you have done that will you become fully effective in giving service to your customers or clients. Before you have done that, you will always be focusing to some degree on each other instead of the team's common goals. There has been much written about group development, so I will not devote more space to it in this book. You can read more about in my book Walk your Talk.[1]

To Agree May Be the Worst Form of Support

It may feel good to talk to a person who agrees with us when we think that someone else has behaved like an idiot. Besides making us feel our frustration and our judgments are legitimate, it can provide a sense of being understood and respected.

There are times, though, when sympathy or being supported might not serve us well. The situations I am mainly thinking of are when we have regular encounters with people we think are challenging. Perhaps there are several people in the working group who have similar opinions about this person and whenever someone is going to meet that person we treat our colleague with sympathy:

"Oh poor you, it's your turn now!"

"Watch out, because he always thinks of something to blame on you."

"I understand if you are nervous, because she never thinks of anyone but herself."

---

[1] Larsson Liv (2017), Walk your Talk.

These types of comments can "freeze" a situation or relationship at a certain place where you cannot see the ways in which you are contributing to aggravating the situation. You want to be supportive of each other, and when the person returns with their complaints, they are received with a "Yes, we already know what kind of person they are." Instead of agreeing you can do some other things:

1. Try to understand your colleague's frustration or anxiety. Don't focus on judgments or labels about someone. Instead, help your colleague to find out what she or he needs.

2. Try to understand what needs your colleague is trying to meet by holding on to a certain view of things. And then, when your colleague is ready, look for the needs in the other person.

3. Explore together whether there might be a solution that can work for both your colleague and for the other party. Look for solutions that can meet everyone's needs, but without giving up on what you value.

> REFLECTION:
> *Which recurring complaints or criticisms are addressed to your organization, your products or your staff?*
> *What needs and wants could be behind them?*
> *Is it in your power to do something about it?*
> *If the power does not lie entirely in your hands, is there anything you can do?*
> *What can you ask for and from whom?*

When we have been through something painful or threatening, it is valuable to be able to talk to someone about it. In some professions or at certain workplaces, supervision or debriefing is a part of the routine after traumatic events. The most common way people manage this is probably through talking to other colleagues. If we do not talk about the traumatic event, it can remain as stress inside us, and "pop up" in situations similar to the one we earlier experienced.

So it may be helpful to schedule talks about such experiences in a routine manner, even when we may not perceive them as very bothersome. I worked for some time with a large organization that had a problem with customer service. When I interviewed the employees in the organization, most of them said that they experienced support from the team they were a part of. I got a chance to see some examples of how much sympathy they showed each other. When they told their colleagues about a problem they had with a customer, they were often supported, and received a pep talk or pity. Sure, they gave each other support – but in a way that often created more distance from the customers.

After the initial interviews, all co-workers received training in listening with empathy. Without any training in how they could respond to their customers, their approach changed radically. They could now hear each other in a way that increased their creativity. They also, to my surprise, found it easier than before to hear what the customers needed, and this led to the service changing in the desired direction. With sympathy, we forget to see all the people's needs as important; with empathy we can support one another without taking sides.

When I worked some years later with another organization with similar problems, I thought I could work by the same plan. But even though they received the same training, not much changed. They received just as many complaints from customers as before and experienced contact with customers as challenging. When we talked about it, it became clear that many of them were so accustomed to getting the sympathy of their colleagues that they continued to hear that, even though their co-workers were just hearing their feelings and needs without taking their side. It was not until we practiced "the dance between honesty and empathy" that there was a change. This taught me that empathy without honesty about how a situation is influencing the listener is often perceived as agreeing or sympathy no matter what the intention has been.

It's Infectious

Just as a satisfied customer can "infect" a work group, a dissatisfied customer can do the same thing. A dissatisfied customer will infect other customers, the employees, and the organization. It can take hours, even days to let go of an upsetting or challenging encounter. In some cases, something that could be called a "culture" tends to form, where people act like they do because it has become a habit and will continue to do so without anyone thinking about it.

REFLECTION:
When something doesn't go the way you or your team had planned, who can you talk to about this?
Have you got any other ways to handle mistakes than to appoint a scapegoat?
Have you thought of a way to learn from your mistakes?

When a mistake leads to guilt or shame, what do you do to cope with these feelings?

Exciting research about mirror neurons show that emotional states are "contagious".[2] We imitate - reflect - each other with mirror neurons in our brain and through them can experience what other people experience. One of my friends, who wanted to inspire a group with these theories, demonstrated this by telling a detailed story about how a person stepped onto a dull rusty rake in such a way that it got stuck in this person's foot. When he got to the part where the person first could not get the rake off of his foot, and then pulled it out with all his strength and with blood pouring out of the foot, people who were listening started making painful faces, covering their ears, and asking him to stop because of the discomfort they felt in their own bodies. Their mirror neurons had presumably become activated in a way that they

---

[2] Bauer, Joachim (2007), Why I Feel What You Feel: Intuitive Communication and the Secret of Mirron Neurons. AmazonCrossing.

concretely experienced the rusty rake-incident.

Joachim Bauer, German professor of immunology, has for example, described knowledge about how we in this way share each other's lives more intimately than we previously have understood. In his book *Why I Feel What You Feel* he writes:

"Mirror neurons implies that people has a common interpersonal space, where they can intuitively understand others' feelings, actions and intentions. They give spontaneous, unconscious information about the emotional state that another person experiences in a certain situation."

I have often wondered how a bad atmosphere could infect us as it is claimed to do. An organization that has most of its focus on what is working and is enjoying this is characterized by celebration and gratitude. Of course I do not mean that we should pretend that everything is fine and dandy if it is not, or that we should "cover" over existing conflicts or injustices. What I am suggesting is that if we consciously direct our attention to things that work and which we appreciate, we will have more energy to deal with the difficult things. It also creates a balance that helps us to see more clearly both what works and what does not.

You have probably noticed that at the times you have received appreciation, it is easier for you in your turn to express appreciation to others. Appreciation is contagious. In both directions.

A customer who gives appreciation contributes to a happy working group, a happy working group contributes to a happy customer. Heart Math Institute in California, suggests how an ability to create coherence between what we think and what we feel not only affects our own physiological state, but also people in our surrounding.[3] When we experience gratitude there is a greater chance that we experience inner coherence. Because it is contagious, we may not only be able to help ourselves, but an entire work group to become more creative and open to new solutions. This, in turn, is useful in connecting situations. Both to create positive ones, but also to solve challenging situations that have arisen.

3 www.heartmath.org

REFLECTION:
Does appreciation from satisfied customers reach out to everyone in your team? Do you have and take time and space to express appreciation for each other?
Do you have any meetings where the focus is on expressing appreciation and paying attention to the things that are working well?

Master Suppression Techniques

In 1976 the social psychologist Berit Ås presented a theory of five master suppression techniques.[4] It was later expanded and reformulated by several different people. I like Elaine Bergqvists words to describe it: "A master suppression technique is a tool that is used to tilt the balance of "equality".[5]

The concept of domination techniques can be described as "strategies of social manipulation by which a dominant group maintains such a position in a (established or unexposed) hierarchy." Ås got the idea for her research of suppression techniques after having attended a number of meetings with men. She discovered that they communicated with each other whenever she was talking in ways that diverted attention from what she wanted to say. She began to imitate these ways, (fetching coffee and beginning to fiddle with something when someone else was talking) and found that it made it easier for her to get her opinions heard. The five master suppression techniques Ås describes in her original theory are:

1. Making someone invisible
2. Ridiculing

---

4 Ås, Berit (2004). "The Five Master Suppression Techniques". In Evengård, Birgitta. Women In White: The European Outlook. Stockholm: Stockholm City Council. pp. 78–83. ISBN 91-631-5716-0.. - Wiki: http://en.wikipedia.org/wiki/Master_suppression_techniques. 17th of March, 2013
5 Bergqvist, Elaine (2008), Härskarteknik. Bokförlaget HörOpp

3. Withholding information

4. Double binding "Damned If You Do And Damned If You Don't".

5. Heaping Blame and Putting to Shame.

Later domination techniques added by Ås (that I have not described below) were:

6. Objectifying

7. Violence/threats of violence

The suppression techniques Ås describes are closely associated with social status within a group. They can be used from a position of disadvantage, but most commonly they are used "top down".

All people and groups can use similar methods, but the concept of master suppression techniques was developed to show how men maintain power over women. Suppression techniques can also be used by women against men, women against women and men against men.

A dilemma with this theory is that when people talk about suppression techniques on a personal level, they are not always relevant. A person may forfeit disclosing important information without it being a suppression technique. A person can tell a joke and it can be perceived as ridiculing without this being the intention. Whether we call a behavior a suppression technique or not, it can be very painful for the person who "suffers" from it. Bergqvist's suggests - "the best approach is not to blame anyone, but to bring the problem out into the open and discuss it" - and I believe we can reach far with that approach.

The theory is useful because it can show someone who has been (or who has seen someone else being) "exposed" to suppression techniques how to "pinpoint" what they saw or experienced. But if we do not distinguish the theory itself and the summing-up interpretations (such as "ridicule") from the actual observations of what has happened, they may contribute to resistance, rather than to change.

I once worked in a workplace where I was not called to a single staff meeting, even though I had worked there for almost a year. Most often, I found out that there would be a meeting, but wondered if I was not wanted there for some reason. When I talked to another person who had worked there for about as long as I had, it appeared that she had had the same experience. She had read about suppression techniques and quickly made the analysis that someone was deliberately withholding information (the third master suppression technique) to dominate us.

At the next meeting, which we both attended, she brought this up (in a not very sensitive way). She presented it as a truth that others deliberately had wanted to withhold information and exclude us, which aroused strong feelings. It took a while to sort out something that could have been quite simple to sort out, something that I now realize having learned more about communication).

The person who had previously taken care of information about these meetings had quit working there two years previously. When she quit, nobody else took her place. There was no structure for how to spread information about the meetings so that everyone heard about them, and it never occurred to anyone that people were not getting this information. Blaming the problem as a matter of suppression techniques, contributed to more pain and frustration than to connection in this situation.

When people do something that can be described as one of these techniques, my assumption is that they either have no connection with their own needs, or that they do not see how the needs can be met with less hurting of others. Most people are not fully aware of using suppression techniques, or at least not about the devastating impact they have on others. They are unaware of how subtle things like tone of voice, or choice of words or body language may seem offensive. And honestly, do you always have total insight of yourself in how you are perceived by others?

I once received a tough lesson on this subject. It all started when I used humor to celebrate something I appreciated. The way I did it was based in a feeling of being comfortable with a certain person. I took it for granted that we could joke about quite serious things because I felt close to her. The other person experienced the joke as a deep insult. I was not attentive to how she felt about this and once I took it so far that our friendship got a severe bump. Only then did I finally understand how I had unknowingly created a power imbalance. Although it was painful for both of us, I learned a much-needed lesson about being more mindful about how I use humor. It has also taught me not to judge others so quickly, even when I see them doing things that seem to hurt others.

If I tread on other people's toes, I hope they could communicate that they are not experiencing having enough space on our common stage. And I hope they could do it in a way that would not alienate me from the community, but would express confidence that I am capable of taking into account the differences in others and giving other people space. Furthermore, I hope they could express themselves in a way that broadens my understanding, by telling me how they experience what is happening. But if they cannot find any ways that are considerate and gentle, I would prefer them to say it in the way they can, so that I can try to take it as the gift it is meant to be.

Since the theory of domination techniques is much talked about (at least in Scandinavia), many participants in our trainings ask for ideas on how to handle these, without answering back in kind and making things worse. They want to know about this, both in relation to colleagues but also with customers.

First, I usually give the advice to regard master suppression techniques as learned and cultural behavior, and to understand that they most often are used unconsciously. They say nothing about the "personality" of the person who uses them. Furthermore, I maintain that it is possible for everyone to become aware of them and change them. The first step is to communicate your concern with the person about which behavior you want to isolate and tell what you have seen.

If master suppression techniques are recurrent in a work group and are perhaps denied, it is effective for a short time to write down specific observations about the behaviors you can see. Then add it to the agenda at a staff meeting and present the observations when there is time to talk about them. In this way it may be less charged than if you point out an observation immediately when you see it. The downside of doing it in this way is that people might not recognize themselves in the description if you cannot be specific with time and place. In that case, you can all agree that the next time someone experiences these kinds of behaviors, he or she, or anyone else who sees it, shall speak up immediately. Many people who are pointed out as using master suppression techniques often feel ashamed and deny it. Therefore, the suppression techniques may need to be talked about on several occasions. The more shame a person feels, the greater the risk that they will deny a behavior that hurts someone else. Therefore, do everything you can to make it clear that the purpose of the conversation is to effect a change, rather than to blame anyone.

I have worked with some work groups that have had these kinds of conversations at meetings where the observations that someone sees as suppression techniques have largely been denied. But these conversations have still had effect and many of the behaviors have subsided. Presumably the feedback did get across but just took some time to process. Remember that it does not need to be the person who has been subjected to a master suppression technique who tells about how it affects him or her. This specific person might feel reluctant to do so, out of fear of being approached in the same way again.

How to deal with the suppression techniques:

1. Making someone invisible

Trying to silence or marginalize people with other views by ignoring them belongs to the category of making someone invisible. Examples of observations:

- Someone speaks up just as you are beginning to talk or picks up what you have just said - as if it was his or her own idea.
- Someone or a few people start moving around, looking through papers, whispering or yawning when you start talking.

What can you do? To bring it up in that actual moment can be scary and leave you feeling vulnerable. It is efficient if you can stick to sharing observations rather than an analysis of what is happening. Find out what their purpose was in doing what they did. It may sound like this:

"When I see you, for the third time, turning towards each other and whispering when I begin to talk, I get confused. I would like to understand what is happening. Michael, would you like to tell me what is going on in you when you do this?"

If you do not finish your observation of someone's behavior with a clear and directed request, the observation will often be met with silence. Somebody has uncovered "the elephant in the room," and the person who has been accused of using a master suppression technique may often perceive him or herself as being attacked, and might become angry, ashamed or remain silent. Even if you manage to stick to the "facts," the other person may still not want to acknowledge what you are pointing out.

But bringing it up can still plant a seed that eventually grows and makes the other person aware of and perhaps willing to change his or her behavior.

Another way to express yourself is to try to gain an understanding of what is going on within the person or the people involved. Then you can start by asking yourself what these people might need? Maybe they are insecure and want to harden themselves to make sure that they can stand up for what they believe in if someone else is persuasive. They may also be nervous because someone wants to make a change that they do not feel safe with. Or they could be worried that if their colleagues are behaving in a certain way, they will lose their place in the community if they do not behave like them.

"Are you worried that everyone's needs, including yours, will not be taken into account by the changes I am proposing? And do you worry that it is not clear how this change would affect a whole lot of people and systems that have taken a long time to build? Is this something close to what is going on inside of you, Matthew?"

Give the person time to think before answering. One might feel vulnerable when asked what one wants, especially after previously having concealed their actions with a suppression technique.

The answer could be spiteful and not very well thought through, and may need to be received with an open mind. Sometimes such a remark will be responded to with yet another suppression technique, such as the second technique, to ridicule.

2. Ridiculing

A person or his or her arguments, appearance, accents or choice of words are portrayed as silly and insignificant. Examples of observations:

- When you have something important to say, a colleague starts laughing and comments on your accent or says that you sound like a person in a funny TV series.

- Someone makes remarks about your appearance in a situation when you are talking about something that you consider important.

You can try to connect to the person by saying something like:
- *Ouch, that hurts. I really want to be heard as this is important to me. Is it clear to you why I want what I say to be taken seriously?*

If you then get the same response, you can bring the incident up at a staff meeting like the one described on page X. It can be useful to tell the person who denied this in advance that you want to bring it up at the next meeting. Not as a threat, but as a kind of preparation so that the person may be more open to feedback. Or maybe you want to ask a third party, for example your supervisor, for help in communicating about this with the concerned person.

Remember, you want to bring it up because you want to see a change and not because you want to blame or shame him or her. The change will be slower if shame and guilt are involved. If you really want to understand the other person, you can also try to say:

"Are these things somewhat embarrassing to talk about and would you want things a bit more easygoing?"

Remember, even if your intention is to really understand, there is a risk that you will be treated the same way again. This is particularly true if you are in a group that has long used "ridiculing" as a way to avoid talking about things that are uncomfortable or around which there is a power struggle.

3. Withholding Information

To exclude someone or reduce his or her role by not providing essential information is the third suppression technique outlined by Ås essential information. Examples of what could happened when someone uses this technique:
- Your colleagues are having a meeting where they talk about

things you are involved in, but to which you have not been invited to take part in.

- Decisions that were supposed to be made at a meeting have already been made earlier in informal settings, to which all concerned participants have not been invited. How to bring up such issues depends on the situation. Maybe you choose to talk to the supervisor or the supervisor of the supervisor about it. Maybe you want to bring it up at a meeting with the entire group, or talk to those who were at the meeting.

If you feel very upset by what has happened it can be valuable to be heard by an outside neutral party before the meeting. The more you can stick to what you have heard, and not mix in interpretations, the better the chance that a change can be achieved. One way to start a conversation might sound like this:

"When I hear that this project plan was agreed on at a meeting I was not invited to, I feel frustrated. I would both like to understand how this has happened and be understood in how it affects my job and me. Does anyone want to tell me how it was that no one invited me to the meeting?"

Here the tone of voice that we say this in is, of course, important. Not that I am suggesting that we try to hide irritation or frustration. But we can be determined without implying that someone has done something wrong or without blaming anyone. What we want is of course to find out what has happened and, if possible, to make sure it does not happen again. If someone feels guilty when they hear the question, they might become defensive, so the last thing you want is for others to feel shame. You want understanding and change so this does not happen again.

4. Double binding

Devaluing and punishing a person regardless of his or her choices of action. Examples of observations:

- If you are thorough with your work assignments and take your time to implement each of them, someone (eg. the boss) regards it as if nothing is getting done. If you do the opposite and speed up, you are told that you are careless.
- A man is accused of not taking responsibility for his home and children; if he does so, he is described as not being masculine.
- A woman who gives priority to staying home with her children instead of going to an evening meeting is described as "flippant" or "not professional enough". If she goes to the meeting, she is told that she is a "bad mother".

If this has become part of how you communicate in your work group, you probably need a few conversations about how to support each other, what kind of values to promote and how to handle differences in the organization. Because there may be different people who criticize various behaviors and the person who is criticized can feel properly "squashed", it is important that he or she gets support to really sort out what has been said, what he or she has heard, and how any trust deficiency can be repaired. You may find the exercise "Prepare" on page 115 useful.

5. Blaming and Shaming

Blaming and shaming is trying to get someone to be ashamed of his or her behavior and attributes, or to imply that what they face is their own fault. This is often done by a combination of ridiculing and double-binding. Examples of observations:

- Although you have not been informed of a meeting, you get to hear, "Well, you should have been active and found out, it is your own fault if you do not keep yourself informed."
- A woman who has experienced sexual abuse is told, "you have yourself to blame, considering what you were wearing".

- You are interrupted several times in the middle of a sentence in a way that your point never gets to be made or that it was made from a different angle.

If the way people communicate leads to shame and guilt, the situations often become quite complex to manage. Maybe it is "infectious" to blame others, maybe this is the way you have been communicating for some time. Sometimes shaming someone is used as a way to experience more power.

Shame

If people are ashamed or feel guilty it adversely affects their willingness to continue communicating. Both shame and guilt make us focus on ourselves. We do everything we can to get away from these unpleasant feelings. This makes us less effective at achieving our goals. When feeling shame we distance ourselves from others in ways that others know nothing about.

A woman came up to me after a seminar I gave on shame. She introduced herself and told me she had hesitated to come and listen, even though I was finally lecturing in her hometown.
"I almost did not dare come to speak to you, but now that I have listened to you speak on shame I really want to tell you what happened to me," she began.

She told me that a few years earlier she had signed up for a course on communication that I was giving. The course was held as an online course and the participants themselves decided the pace they wanted to study at. She had paid for it and finished the first exercise. Then because of a lack of time she did not continue the course. She had not informed me of this but just dropped out. The thought of coming to the seminar had made her feel so much shame that she hesitated to come because she wanted to avoid the discomfort, without knowing at the time it was actually shame she was feeling and trying to avoid. She realized that I did not know what she looked like, and thus she would be able to come to the seminar and determine there if she wanted to reveal herself or not.

She was relieved when she realized that she had hesitated to come to the seminar because she wanted to avoid shame:

"It is so embarrassing not to complete things, especially if you do not communicate anything about it. I had thought about getting in touch but it just never happened."

She went on to celebrate the realization of how much choice she was now experiencing. When she was not trying to get rid of the shame, she was no longer controlled by it. I did not know that this had been going on within her. Her choice not to pursue the course had not affected me any other way than that I had occasionally wondered how come she had not continued the course. I felt glad that she had approached me and dared to show her vulnerability. One of my motivations behind writing one of previous books, *Anger, Guilt and Shame, Reclaiming Power and Choice*, was that I started to see how people perceive more choice when they have the tools to deal with shame.[6]

This woman's story reminded me of times when I, for various reasons, have been ashamed and tried to manage it by avoiding people or situations. Sometimes others have interpreted me as cold, sometimes as indifferent. Most of the time it has only been me who has suffered from limiting my living space and my freedom of choice. For example, I have noticed I hesitate entering a store or a restaurant where I once felt embarrassment or shame. This hesitation has made it clear to me how important it is to respond to customers or clients in a way that minimizes the risk of provoking shame and helps everyone keep their dignity.

Below, the four directions we usually move in when we want to avoid feeling shame, are summarized. Learning to recognize them is valuable as we are then more likely to handle them in a way that is supportive for us. It will also make it easier for us to support others in handling shame or embarrassment.

---

6 Larsson, Liv (2013) Anger guilt and shame. Reclaiming Power and Choice. Friare Liv.

1. We withdraw, either physically or mentally.

2. We criticize ourselves and blame our actions and ourselves if something goes wrong.

3. We rebel against the shame by showing that we certainly do not feel ashamed nor agree to be stepped on.

4. We criticize and blame others for misunderstandings or mistakes that have occurred and we might get really angry.

REFLECTION:
Do you recognize that you sometimes use one of the strategies above? In what situations does this happen and what do you feel and need then? Is there any other way you would rather act in these situations?

Do you think some of the behaviors described above are difficult to manage or understand, when you experience them in others?

Regardless of whether I myself am ashamed or another person I want to connect with is ashamed, it can be a challenge to manage the situation. If I am the one who is ashamed, the most effective way to deal with it is to first of all, admit it to myself. Then I can find out what I need in that moment. If it is the person I am encountering who is ashamed, she or he often needs to be received in a way that is perceived as respectful and does not further increase the shame.

When we have created that kind of connection, it is easier to find strategies to move forward in a way that includes everyone's needs.

If we try to ignore the feeling of shame and just quickly go to solutions, it can work, but often only in the short term - at least if it feels like a "cover-up". The risk that we lose a customer in this way is highly likely. When they feel the shame "lurking in some corner," ready to pop up as soon as they come closer to us in some way, they are very likely not to return or use our services again.

Chapter 5

To Say "No" and Maintain Connection

I want to be able to tell people to go to hell in such a way that they look forward to the trip!
- REQUEST OF A COURSE PARTICIPANT

If it is important for us to always be liked, we risk getting in trouble if we are in an organization where we sometimes need to say "no" to someone.

But there is a difference between "saying no" and "saying no". Therefore, I am devoting this entire chapter to how we can say "no" while protecting the connection to the other person. A customer who gets a "no" will perhaps be dissatisfied, but what is crucial is whether they are willing to come back, or after my "no" shun me and the organization I work for, like the plague.

The fear of hearing a "no" can make it challenging to express clear requests. At the same time, when we are not clear about what we want, we seem to be more often at risk of hearing a "no."

But what exactly is it that makes it so terrible to hear a "no?" One of the reasons that it may be difficult to express requests is that we have learned that if someone says no to what we are asking for, it says something about us. We have learned to interpret a "no" as a rejection.

To avoid the shame of not being worthy of a "yes," we stop asking for what we need, or hide our desires behind vague wording. Sometime this situation flips over and people who have grown tired of holding back their requests begin to demand and threaten, in the belief that this will give them what they need.

For the same reasons we often avoid saying no. We want to

acknowledge people (especially those who are close to us), and are afraid that they will associate us with someone who devalues them, if we say no to their requests.

But when someone says, "yes" without meaning it, there will usually, sooner or later, be an "invoice" due. And for those who did not know that the other person said "yes," but wanted to say "no", it can feel tough to be asked to "pay for something you did not even know that you bought".

REFLECTION:
What are you most afraid will happen if you get a "no" from a person who is "important" to you?

What are you most afraid will happen if you say "no" to a person who is "important" to you?

Because hearing a "no" is often challenging, a person might come out of a situation where he or she received a "no" with a "bitter aftertaste" in his or her mouth. It may even end up with the person not coming back. It could also lead to that person "backbiting" the organization and, worse, spreading lies or inaccurate images of it. Therefore, it is valuable for everyone in an organization to be able to say "no" and to do it in a way that preserves the connection with the person they say "no" to.

When we hear a "no" we usually want one of the below:

- To be understood in how frustrating and painful it can be to get a no for an answer.
- To understand what lies behind the 'no' (often, that wish occurs only after we have been understood).

We would like to hear the reasons for a "no" with such clarity that we realize we ourselves might also say no in a similar situation. Referring to company policies when someone is already upset will, in most cases, stir up more upset and thus get in the way of connection and maybe co-operation.

One of my course participants realized that if he did not fully understand the company's policy, it was more difficult for him to take the dialogue further with a customer. He noticed that when he was unsure of whether he actually agreed with the policy or not, he became even more firm in his "no" to the customers request. When he explored this further, he realized that when he stood behind a policy and it was congruent with his values he felt safer in deepening a conversation about the issue. He could even engage when someone was deeply questioning the policy or his way of implementing it. In situations where he personally did not stand behind the decision, he put up a strong facade not to show his insecurity due to concerns about making the situation worse.

Sometimes people mix up our willingness to contribute with our possibility to do just that in a certain situation. They say or think:

"If you really wanted to help me, you would say 'yes' to what I am asking for."

This confusion is usually solvable if we both listen to how disappointed people are and make it clear to them that we would like to help but actually cannot find a way to do it according to company policy.

The staff at a conference center I was working with had undergone a period of many conflicts. It had led to several of the staff going on sick leave. The absence of their colleagues led to greater stress among those who remained. That in turn led to more misunderstandings and conflicts. No one knew how to start dealing with the conflicts.

One thing we discovered was that the person who handled the bookings often said yes to groups, even though there was really no room for them, nor enough staff. He often said yes to things that the staff asked for, even though his yes posed more problems for other people in the staff. When we confronted him, he at first became frustrated but then burst out saying:

"But the management has asked us to always be nice and say yes".
Probably the management had in their desire to contribute to customers conveyed the notion that good service meant to always say yes. However, a "no" can implement better service than a "yes" which one cannot live up to. A valuable formulation could be:

"I'm worried that if I say yes to this, it will have these consequences ... Now when you hear this, do you still wish to hear a yes to what you are asking for, or does what I'm saying change your request in any way?"

Three Useful Assumptions

When someone says no to us, we can benefit from the below three assumptions. These assumptions may help us find solutions that can meet both our own and others people's needs.

1. Behind every "no" there is a "yes" to something else.

If we ask someone for help with something and the person says "no," we can remind ourselves that she or he probably does not see how a "yes" would meet her or his needs.
It tends to be easier to continue the dialogue if we first focus on what this person would like to say yes to. Perhaps the person needs to rest, to feel free to choose or to have peace to complete something that is important for them.

2. A "no" is an invitation to further dialogue.

We can continue the dialogue after receiving a "no" by asserting that we understand that the other person has a reason to say no. Since we still want our need for support to be met, we can continue to communicate. Here it is important that we take into consideration the needs of the other person.

Example:

"I hear that you have a need to finish what you are doing in order to keep your promises. At the same time, I have a big need for support. I wonder if you can talk to me for five minutes about how we can ensure both that you will be able to finish what you are doing and that I get the support I need for this task?"

Maybe we still get a no, and in that case the third assumption is useful. Doing that, we still strive for what we need, but not at the expense of connection.

3. There are always several ways to get a need met.

When we hear that the other person is not willing to give up on finishing what he or she is doing, we can think about whether there are other ways to get our need for support met. For example we might ask someone else for help. But if, for some reason, we really want this particular person's support, we can propose a strategy that we believe will satisfy both this person's needs as well as ours:

"I wonder if there is anything I can do that can help you free up some time so that you can both help me and get your project finished?"

No matter how we choose to act we can, by taking in the third assumption and being open to shifting strategies, find a way to meet everyone's needs. The clarity in this usually increases when we really take in both sides' needs and keep them equally important. The creativity that is released when we are no longer stuck in a certain strategy can help us see solutions we have not seen before.

When we say no ourselves, we can benefit from thinking in the same way:

1. Behind every "no" there is a "yes" to something else.

When you say no, make it clear what it is that you are saying yes to with your no. That is, what values are you trying to protect and what needs are you trying to meet. If you do this, it is often easier for other people to not take your "no" as criticism or as a rejection.

2. A "no" is an invitation to further dialogue.

Even if you have said no to a request that someone else has expressed, you want to continue being connected to him or her. Perhaps you would like to suggest continuing the dialogue at a later time. Remember however, that continuing the dialogue right away is what often creates the most connection, at least if the communication is respectful and doesn't feel forced or mandatory.

Perhaps the person has asked for something that you do not know how to say yes to, because you have a policy or values that are in opposition to it. Then it is usually connecting to make these reasons clear to the other person.

3. There are always several ways to get a need met.

You want to remember that the other person has needs that you want to meet, but not necessarily in the way that the person has suggested. Make sure the other person knows that you really want them to be satisfied without having to give something up, and you can create a better possibility that will satisfy your both.

To hone your skills in saying no but stay connected, do the exercise on page 160.

Guilt

We experience guilt when part of us wants to say "no" to another's request, yet another part of us think that we should say "yes", We understand that if we say "yes," it will contribute to meeting the other person's needs. At the same time this "yes" will not fully contribute to meeting our own needs. What remains is an ambivalence that leaves a gnawing uneasiness in us.

Guilt is a sign that we care, but also that we are not creative enough to think "outside the box." Creativity is kidnapped by "either-or" thinking. It is either you who will get what you need, or the other person. As thinking like this caused the problem in the first place, if we continue to think in this way we will probably never solve the problem. The thoughts spin faster and faster and the thread of thoughts become more and more entangled while we continue thinking.

Sometimes we get so tired of trying to sort through all the thoughts that we just act. If we give in and say, "yes" to the other person's request, the feelings of guilt usually disappear or diminish. But while we first experience a relief, we might later become bitter or angry. We might get irritated if we think that the other person does not show enough gratitude that we have given up what we ourselves wanted. We might think, "next time it will be my turn," and the other person now owes me. And if at some later point we make a request to them and they say no, this could be the start of a messy situation.

If we have neglected important values in the process, some of us will become depressed or lose our zest for life. Nothing feels fun and we can hardly remember what it was that was so important to us. It is almost as if we do not dare to continue hoping and standing up for our dreams. In either case, both we, the other person, and our relationship, will suffer, especially if this is a recurring pattern. If we want to make sure to create stable relationships we want to also make sure our "yes" is truly a "yes" from our heart.

How do we get out of a destructive guilt loop? One way is

to actually go to the heart of the matter and find the different needs that are fighting for our attention. On the one hand, maybe I need to contribute or to experience love. On the other hand, maybe I need freedom, autonomy or creativity. When I really am connected with these needs, not just on the thought level, but when I wholeheartedly feel that they are important, something almost magical takes place. I become creative and often I suddenly see solutions that had always been right there in front of me, but which I somehow had missed.

Trust Can be Built

The first step in creating connection is to create such a quality of contact that we understand when and how we can help other people with what they ask for. With a strong connection we will be able to say "no" to what they ask for. At the same time, we will help them to find other ways to meet their needs if we can.

If the first step is about creating a strong connection, the next step is about building trust that we can actually do what we claim we can do. Stephen Covey, in his book *The Speed of Trust,* connects the sense of trust with increased effectivity.[1]

When everything does not need to be double-checked and inspected and when we keep our agreements, we can focus on our goals. Covey says that when we have trust in each other, we save both time and energy. He describes what is needed for trust to occur in four points.

1. Integrity

For many people, integrity is associated with trust. Integrity sometimes means honesty, but for me it is more than that. It has to do with what we say we can do. And to say "no" to things we know or anticipate that we cannot do. When a person does not experience full integrity behind what someone has said or done it often leads

---

[1] Covey, Stephen M R (2008), The Speed of Trust - the one thing that changes everything. Simon & Schuster.

to broken trust. It could be that someone has not completed what he or she said that he or she would do. It can also be about the way an agreement has been broken.

2. Intention.

Trust is built when our intention is clear to other people. No matter what action it is about, an understanding of what lies behind the decision is crucial for connection. If someone thinks that we have a "hidden agenda," he or she easily becomes suspicious and hears malicious intention in everything we say and do.

Over a short period of time I was once involved in two conversations in which two different persons were acting in ways that were challenging for me. In both occasions these persons asked me some questions, which I knew they in fact already had the answers to. In two of the situations, it was about persons they "pretended" they did not know. In the third case, it was about a different kind of information.

On all three occasions, I was so surprised that I did not know how I would bring it up. I had the thought that I was being inspected and controlled. It provoked discomfort and affected my trust in these people. It was somewhat easier when I realized that they probably wanted to hear my views, and thought that if I did not know that they knew these persons, they would get a more honest standpoint from me.

If they had been open about what they knew from the beginning and had asked me how this affected me, my trust in them would probably have grown instead of turning into the discomfort I felt. It would have led to more transparency and more clarity about how we could work together in the future. It taught me once again how important both honesty and mutual trust are in connecting to others.

3. Competence, skills and knowledge.

Knowledge and clarity about what skills we have is part of what makes other people trust us. If I am sick, I do not go to a garage to get well and if my car is broken, I do not drive to a health center to get it repaired.

Knowing where our boundaries are is also a kind of competence. This means that we are more easily able to act with integrity, say "no" if necessary, and only promise the results we know we are able to deliver.

4. Result.

If we have the knowledge and intention, but do not generate results, it will be more difficult for others to trust that we can keep our promises. To show that we can generate results is a way to repair trust that has been previously broken. It does not mean that we expect the other person to immediately experience trust just because this time we created results. It may take some time to repair old disappointments.

What can we do if someone does not trust us? No matter who it is, it rarely helps to ensure that we certainly are reliable. To think or say that they "should trust us" often has the opposite effect and can lead to suspicions about why you are pushing this trust issue so strongly. Most often, action is needed to build trust. So instead of trying to convince the other party that we are reliable, we can show that we are willing to contribute to the other party's trust in us. For example, we can say, "I wonder what I could do that would help you to have more trust in me?"

When the person then asks for something, consider if you can say yes to what she or he asks for with integrity and then make sure to follow through. That is how trust can be built.

"You cannot talk yourself out of a problem you behaved yourself into."[2]
COVEY

I found some thought provoking research about trust that showed that, contrary to what the researchers had assumed, those

[2] Covey, Stephen M R (2008), The Speed of trust - the one thing that changes everything. Simon & Schuster.

who believe that other people generally are honest and reliable, make better "lie detectors" than those who say that people are not reliable.[3]

I suppose that for people who assume that it is possible to trust that others are honest, it is easier also to notice signs when this is not the case. Perhaps they also "listen to these signs," say no to things they do not want, thus getting "cheated" less often, and therefore perceive that people can be trusted.

3. http://www.sciencedaily.com/releases/2010/08/100813090457.htm

Chapter 6

Preparing for Connection

Preparing for challenging conversations and meetings is valuable, even if we cannot control what will happen during one. When we prepare for a conversation, we may emphasize the subject, *what* we are going to talk about, and less on *how* to talk to the other person. It is often useful to do the opposite.

Content:

Both "What" and "How" will affect the outcome. For example, what is to be discussed, proposals that are made, which tasks to perform. These things are often more visible than the process going on in the meantime.

The Process:

For example, how people talk to each other, how decisions about what to do are made, how they feel about their cooperation, how committed and involved everyone experiences themselves as well as their coworkers.

To clarify what we think about the other person, what we feel about meeting with him or her and what we want to happen in and through the meeting gives us more grounding in ourselves. Furthermore, taking a moment to reflect on how this meeting might feel for the other person can help us to "see the human being" behind what we might otherwise just hear as demands. When we do that, even a hard case will be easier, because we can talk about it in a way that we can be proud of afterwards.

Everybody experiences situations that are challenging. Learning to recognize them is a first step. The next step is to practice new ways of communicating in those circumstances where we easily lose our footing. Just like an athlete who is training for a competition, we can practice communicating in situations that we want to work better.

REFLECTION:

What kind of situations are particularly challenging for you?

What behavior can make you lose your footing?

What can you hear someone say that is challenging for you to connect with?

What Might be Challenging for You?

You can prepare for meetings that are challenging in different ways. It may be a preparation for a specific meeting that you know you will have in the near future. You can also prepare for meetings that in general tend to be challenging, as you cannot predict when they will occur. In the second case you might, for example, want to practise on connecting to:

- One dissatisfied angry person.
- A dissatisfied group of angry people.
- A person who previously has made demands.
- A person you have so far experienced as difficult to reach.
- A person you have strong judgments about, which you have not expressed.
- A person you have strong judgments about, which you have expressed.
- Someone you want to say "no" to.
- Someone you worry about hearing a "no" from.
- Someone you worry will say "yes," even though she or he does not intend to pursue what you are asking for.

- Someone you worry will ask you to "think positive" no matter what the situation is.

- Someone you think is going to blame you or another person that you work with.

- Someone who has threatened, for example, to go to the press or to your boss if you do not do what she or he wants.

- Someone who has threatened to resort to violence and harm you, a colleague, a family member, a child or someone else.

- Someone who has expressed strong dissatisfaction about a decision you have been involved in and you want to stand behind.

- Someone who is sad and just wants to give up.

- Someone who expresses him or herself with irony, sarcasm or with mixed messages in other ways.

Use the questions on the following page to handle the situations above, or to prepare for a specific meeting.

Prepare

1. What intentions do you have with this meeting, letter, message or phone call? What results would you like to achieve through it?

2. What do you feel at the thought of this conversation?

3. How do you want to feel afterwards?

4. What do you think the person you are going to connect with feels before your meeting? What do you think he or she needs?

5. Are you clear about what the other person wants to get out of your meeting?

6. Is there any information you might find useful before the meeting?

7. Is there any practical preparation you can do beforehand?

Prepare For Connection by E-mail or Phone

When we connect with others by telephone or e-mail, the situation is different from when we meet them face-to-face. There is a lot of research about whether it is the choice of words or the body language that determines how much of a message is perceived. The words we use certainly affect our communication but so do body language, facial expressions, emotions and gestures. When we do not see each other there are different misunderstandings than when we are sitting in the same room. Therefore, we need to prepare ourselves a little differently before a telephone conference. When we use e:mail, we miss even the tone of voice, which can further contribute to misunderstandings.

There are advantages with communicating by phone or e-mail. For example, preconceptions based on someone's appearance are minimized when we do not see the person and have not met him or her before. It may also feel safer, because the person cannot harm us physically. However we run the risk of missing the important emotional messages found in body language when we communicate through written word. In a telephone call, we get information by the person's tone of voice and variation in tone but we miss the things that gestures can convey. Irony, sarcasm and fuzzy requests often create misunderstandings. This is particularly true when we communicate by phone or e-mail.

Prepare For a Phone Call

I have noticed that my phone calls are more effective and usually shorter when I properly prepare for them. Essentially the same preparation as when I meet a person face to face also applies to phone calls:

- What do I want?

- What do I feel?

- What do I need?

What do I think the other person is feeling and needing and what he or she wants to get out of our meeting? Are there any facts or information that would be useful for me to know in advance?

Before I call, I ask myself:

Is a phone call the best way to communicate, especially if it is something emotionally charged that we will be talking about?

- Maybe I want to meet the person instead?

Then I think about:

- What is the overall purpose of the call?

- What requests do I have?

- What do I want from this call?

When I start the conversation, I often start by expressing my requests, so that the other person knows where I am coming from and where I want to go.

I also prepare by writing down:

- What do I feel about this conversation?

- What has happened that makes me feel this way? (Here I distinguish between what I think has happened and the clear observations I have made of what actually has happened.)

- What do I need in relation to this?

- Can I ask someone else for something that can help me to get what I need?

- What do I think the other person feels and needs before a conversation with me?

- What do I think she or he wants by a meeting with me?

We might not communicate any of this but the more aware we are of what affects us, the less it will control us unconsciously.

To Communicate Something Emotionally Charged Via Phone

If you are going to convey something emotionally charged by phone, give yourself plenty of time to get clear about what you want from the call. What do you want the result to be? Is it reasonable? What is needed to achieve this? If you want to practice, you can start by writing down one or more observations you want to talk to someone about.

Write down what is the reason behind your wanting to communicate. Be careful to distinguish between interpretations and observations. Expressing an observation may be to quote what someone says or to describe what you have seen a person do. You do it without claiming that you know what his or her intentions were. Make sure it is a quote that the person hopefully will recognize. The purpose of this is to create a common platform for what you want to talk about. It may be, for example:

"At the meeting yesterday, I heard you say," 'This is stupid, and you really don't get anything.'

Express no analysis of what you think about this and express no thoughts about what the person should have done differently. Refrain from saying anything about what you think was his or her intention. Instead, talk about what you are feeling and needing right now. You can continue like this and try to imagine what went on in the other person:

"When you said this, did you feel disappointed because you wanted someone to hear how important it is for you to get support in this?" You can also continue by expressing what you feel and need: "When I think about it, I feel confused and anxious and I would like to understand more about what you meant and what you want".

If you choose the latter, make sure to end with a request about what you now want to hear from the other person. Some examples might be:

"So, I was wondering if you would like to tell me something about what you need in relation to this right now, and if there is anything I can do to contribute to that?"

or,

"Before I hear anything about what actually happened, I would like to hear something about how you feel now about me bringing this up."

If the person does not answer:

If the person does not answer and if it is very important, you can consider what you want to say in the person's voice mail if he or she does not answer. What request do you want to express to a secretary? Do you want to say that you will get in touch or ask him or her to contact you? Do you want to give a specific time when it is easiest to reach you?

Remember!

Remember that if you work at an authority or organization that can seem daunting for those who contact you, the call with you may be challenging. People may shy away, be quieter, over explain, or be more or less polite just because of the title you have, or the organization you work for. They may have taken a defensive position or a defensive attitude even before you have made contact.

E-mail that Create Connection

Communicating via e-mail has clear limitations, but is becoming more and more common. Therefore, it is valuable to pay close attention to how you write an e-mail message. In principle, the same approach as when you meet a person applies here. Prepare yourself by asking yourself what intentions you have with this communication. What do you want? What do you think the other person feels and needs when you contact him or her?

The difference with e-mail is that you cannot see faces or gestures or hear the tone when someone is communicating. To make a joke is often difficult because irony or hints are not always understood, so be cautious with this if you do not know the other person well.

Remember that everything that is written in an e-mail message can easily be forwarded and made public. One benefit of e-mail is that you can change what you have written several times, twisting and turning words to really achieve what you want to say. With this in mind, I suggest that you ask yourself these questions when you are writing an e-mail:

Is an e-mail the best way to communicate this? If there is something emotionally charged that you are writing about, it might be better to call or meet with the person instead. The same is true if there are many difficult pieces in what you want to communicate. It may be easier to meet if you suppose that what you want to communicate about will raise many questions.

It is usually better to write in shorter paragraphs and convey pieces of information one piece at a time, or try to understand one person at a time if it is a message to an e-mail group. How can you make the message as short as possible?

Wait to send the next piece until you have received confirmation that the first thing you wanted to communicate has been understood or was a correct reflection of what they said. When we try to communicate several things at the same time, there are often misunderstandings or something gets left out.

Ask yourself:

What have I actually seen the other person do or heard the other person say?

Make sure to distinguish between interpretations and observations. It usually works better to quote people than to do an analysis of why they said what they said. For example:

"When I heard you say you do not want to work with us anymore because we are not competent enough..."

Instead of:

"When you criticize us and accuse us of not doing our jobs."

It is of course important that the person recognizes that he or she actually said what you are quoting, so you may also want to provide the time and place. Add:

"This is what I heard you say..." or, "I do not know if I remember it word for word, but I remember it like this...".

This is to make clear to the other person that you want to create connection and understanding and not just "be right".

How do I want the other person to act now? Finish the e-mail with a clear request. What you want the person to do when she or he has read your message. If you have written a long message it may be useful to also express this request in the beginning so that people know that before they read the e-mail. Is there any risk that what I write will be perceived as an attack, as blaming, demands or threats, or as if it is meant to make others feel ashamed?

If what you write is emotionally charged, read the text again before you send it. Minimize the risk that the recipient will hear what you write as an accusation, that you blame, demand or threaten. Send it only if you think you have done everything you can to make your message sound like a request for continued dialogue.

Chapter 7

The Inner Work

Already in the previous chapters, I have discussed how we can prepare for different situations by being clear about what is going on within us. In this chapter I want to explore this a little more. Central to the mental work is learning to manage self-criticism. Learning to cope with disappointment, guilt, shame or anger about things that did not work out as we had planned.

I have discussed how we can prepare for different situations by being clear about what is going on within us in previous chapters. In this chapter I want to explore this a little more.

One aspect of inner work is learning to manage self-criticism, whether it is stimulated by something someone else said or just by your own thoughts.

Learning to cope with self-criticism as we feel disappointment, guilt, shame or anger about things that did not work out as we had planned, will enable us to go forward and let go when we find an underlying "lesson."

Seeing ourselves as a human beyond what we may perceive as stupid choices or an unacceptable approach, is a key ingredient in order to be available for connection to others.

A step in this direction is to listen inwardly, to hear what our "good reason" was in a situation we think we failed in, and to understand what needs we were trying to meet. This can begin when we are willing to accept all critical and judgmental thoughts about others and ourselves without censoring them.

NOTE! Do not shout your thoughts out loud but keep them to yourself until you have examined them. Try to accept, or at least listen to these thoughts even if they are violent in their nature.

Accepting our way of thinking (the way we have learned to think) tends to make it easier to have compassion for ourselves. The internal struggle no longer takes all our attention and we may eventually find new solutions.

It is important not to express judgmental thoughts out loud, nor to believe in the content of those thoughts. Nevertheless, it is valuable to embrace them and try to understand what they are trying to tell us. The next step is for us to remind ourselves that behind all judgments we can find feelings and needs. You can go deeper in this challenge using the exercise on page 154.

Chapter 8

Threats

Queen Victoria and Prince Albert had an argument, which some-times happens in a marriage. One word led to another and suddenly Prince Albert left the room with a firm step and a frown and locked himself in his studio.

Queen Victoria ran after him, knocked on the door and said in a loud voice, "Open!" No answer. She banged on the door and shouted, "open immediately!" No answer. She shouted at the top of her lungs, "I am the Queen of England, Scotland, Wales and Ireland, Empress of India, and the whole British Empire, Supreme Commander of the British Armed Forces and I hereby order you to open the door!"

No answer. Finally she said in a soft voice: "Albert, I'm sorry, I love you and miss you." The door opened.

Do you remember a situation when something that could have been very simple, was made more difficult because the communication between people was not working? When a "molehill became a mountain" and everyone afterwards wondered how it could have gotten so out of hand? Meetings where afterwards you could see that the opinions of the participants really were not so different at all, but where the conflict began to resemble a war, rather than an attempt to cooperate? Where threats were perhaps spoken or just "hung in the air?"

Although few of us experience threats in our everyday lives, they tend to leave marks that stay for a long time. They can lead to a psychological tension that affects us both physically and mentally. After a threatening situation, it is useful to talk to someone about it, perhaps together with the entire workgroup. Sometimes it can be useful to have a "debriefing" in the group.

From Small Conflict to Threats

Almost always, threats are preceded by a conflict that has escalated. One way to describe this escalation is to imagine that conflicts have different levels. At the first level, we, as a part of a conflict, have the ability to remember both our own needs, the needs of the other person, plus what the conflict is about. We are upset, but still want the other person to be happy with the solution.

A common reason for a conflict to escalate to the next level is that neither party listens and takes in the reality of the other person, nor has the ability to show the other person that they are doing so. It is still clear to us that we want to deal with the problem, but it is hard to take in how our actions may influence the other person. Or maybe we are acting out of fear that the other person will not take our needs into account and that we will not be satisfied with the result.

An equally common reason is that someone gives up her or his own needs and interests, even though it does not feel right. If, for example, there has been a loud discussion, it may be that one party gives priority to harmony, acceptance, love or kindness, rather than standing up for their own interests. In relationships that extend over a long period of time this can become a game where the biggest martyr "wins" and where intimacy and trust suffer.

Conflicts can escalate to yet another level if the parties cannot find a way to consider each other's needs to a greater extent. At this point not even the solution of the problem is important anymore. This is about survival, about showing that we will not give up and that we might consider revenge or some kind of punishment to express our frustration and anger.

Fortunately, for most of us, it is not very often that conflicts escalate to the last level described above, in our daily lives. To prevent a conflict from escalating, at least one party, or possibly a third party, needs to focus on taking everyone's needs into account. When the parties feel that the needs of both sides are important, it is more likely that they will want to cooperate and the conflict can be scaled down. Knowing how to "downsize a conflict" is valuable knowledge when it comes to situations where threats, demands or a rising frustration have appeared. Threats need not be only about direct violence, they may also be threats about smearing someone, about going to the media or the manager or making something about the other person public in some other way.

The most effective tool in downsizing a conflict is to listen. And this is not just being quiet so that it is clear to the other person that we are indeed interested in understanding his or her point of view. It is about listening for the "right stuff," i.e. that which is the essence of what the other person wants to be heard and to then be able to reproduce what we have heard them say. We want to be able to listen to others without taking what they say personally or giving up things that are important to us. To connect what someone feels to what she or he needs makes it easier to avoid hearing what someone says as criticism.

If we do not want to listen, we can choose to express ourselves. In a difficult situation, it is more important than ever to know how to express ourselves in a way that minimizes the risk of escalating the conflict. Here timing is also important. When someone is in a strong affective mode, they usually tend to hear criticism even if we express ourselves carefully.

In order to continue to communicate and connect we need to downsize the conflict. Anything that can be perceived as explanations, denials, defenses or attacks risks adding fuel to the fire of conflict. Words such as "but," and "not my fault," but also labels such as "dominant", "selfish", and "disrespectful," are all risky in these situations. What usually works better is to express what "we" feel, what "we" need and what "we" want, as vulnerably, honestly and overtly as possible, and without talking about other people and their intentions. And of course it is important to listen.

Sometimes we cannot find a way to downsize the conflict and then, of course, we need to act to protect ourselves or other people. When we act with the intent to protect, it is useful to have the clarity that our intention really is to protect and not to punish. If we want to punish the other person, we will act from a place of anger, which can make the situation worse. If a threatening situation arises and we want to end the dialogue in a safe way, it is often useful, if possible, to end it together with a third person. We can move to another room where there is a colleague or ask someone to join us. It can reduce the degree of threat or at least we can protect ourselves.

In some organizations, it has been decided that if someone receives a threat via the telephone, the call will be terminated at once to protect the people involved. The dilemma here is that sometimes threats are hidden and not direct.

Maybe there is no threat to harm you, your property, the company or your children, but instead the other person is threatening to harm him- or herself. The person calling or visiting you might say,

"I don't seem to be getting anywhere, so I see no other choice than to commit suicide!"

These are obviously very challenging situations comprised of many levels. In some cases it may help to take the extra time to listen, perhaps saying something like,

"It sounds like this is really tough for you, I wonder if I can help you call someone who can help you to sort this out?"

Remember that a proposal for someone to talk to a psychologist or a doctor can be provocative in itself. Make it clear that you are wanting them to speak to someone in an effort to be supportive and not as an analysis of the person's mental health condition.

Using Power to Protect

If we want to use our power or physical strength, an important question to ask our self is,

"Am I intervening to protect or to punish someone?"

When I intervene or act with the intention to punish, it often has negative consequences. One way to determine if I am intervening to punish, is to see if I am using language that suggests that the other person has done something wrong and deserves to be punished for this. In these situations I often say or do things that I will later regret.

If I act with the intention to protect, I will do what is needed, because I know where my "limits" are. My actions will not contain criticism and I will not use violence. I can hold someone who might hurt themselves or somebody else, but I am aware that I am doing it in order to protect and not to "make them realize that they have done something wrong."[1]

Sudden threats

In the previous text, I focused on threats that arise step by step in escalated conflicts.

Threats can also appear suddenly. Even in the most threatening of situations, listening might actually work to downsize the conflict. Read about Maria who had understood the possibilities of empathic listening. Prior to the violent situation described, she had participated in a course in NVC. Among other things, she had learned how difficult it is for a person who is upset to hear a "but..." after a question or after asking for something. She recounted the following story during a second course in NVC with Marshall Rosenberg. It is taken from his book Nonviolent Communication, A Language of Life[2]. The incident took place during a night shift at a detoxification clinic in Toronto.

At eleven o'clock one night, a few weeks after her first NVC training, a man who'd obviously been taking drugs walked in off the street and demanded a room. The young woman started to explain to him that all the rooms had been filled for the night. She was about to hand the man the address of another detox center when he hurled her to the ground.

---

1 Read more about this in *Cracking the Communication Code* (2015) Hoffmann & Larsson. Friare Liv.
2 Rosenberg, Marshall (2007), *Nonviolent Communication , A Language of Life* . Puddle Dancer Press.

"Next thing I knew, he was sitting across my chest holding a knife to my throat and shouting, 'You bitch, don't lie to me! You do too have a room!'"

She then proceeded to apply her training by listening for his feelings and needs. "You remembered to do that under those conditions?" I asked, impressed.

"What choice did I have? Desperation sometimes makes good communicators of us all! You know, Marshall," she added, "that joke you told in the workshop really helped me. In fact, I think it saved my life."

"What joke?"

"Remember when you said never to put your 'but' in the face of an angry person? I was all ready to start arguing with him; I was about to say, 'But I don't have a room!' when I remembered your joke. It had really stayed with me because only the week before, I was arguing with my mother and she'd said to me, 'I could kill you when you answer "but" to everything I say!' Imagine, if my own mother were angry enough to kill me for using that word, what would this man have done? If I'd said, 'But I don't have a room!' when he was screaming at me, I have no doubt he would have slit my throat.

"So instead, I took a deep breath and said, 'It sounds like you're really angry and you want to be given a room.'

He yelled back, 'I may be an addict, but by God, I deserve respect. I'm tired of nobody giving me respect. My parents don't give me respect. I'm gonna get respect!' I just focused on his feelings and needs and said, 'Are you fed up, not getting the respect that you want?'"

"How long did this go on?" I asked.

"Oh, about another thirty-five minutes," she replied.

"That must have been terrifying."

"No, not after the first couple of interchanges, because then something else we'd learned here became apparent. When I concentrated on listening for his feelings and needs, I stopped seeing him as a monster. I could see, just as you'd said, how people who seem like monsters are simply human beings whose language and behavior sometimes keep us from seeing their humanness. The more I was able to focus my attention on his feelings and needs, the more I saw him as a person full of despair whose needs weren't being met. I became confident that if I held my attention there, I wouldn't be hurt. After he'd received the empathy he needed, he got off me, put the knife away, and I helped him find a room at another center."

Delighted that she'd learned to respond emphatically in such an extreme situation, I asked curiously, "What are you doing back here? It sounds like you've mastered NVC and should be out teaching others what you've learned."

"Now I need you to help me with a hard one," she said.

"I'm almost afraid to ask. What could be harder than that?"

"Now I need you to help me with my mother. Despite all the insight I got into that 'but' phenomenon, you know what happened? At supper the next evening when I told my mother what had happened, she said, 'You're going to cause your father and me to have a heart attack if you keep that job. You simply have to find different work!' So guess what I said to her? 'But, mother, it's my life!'"

Chapter 9

System and Individual in Interaction

A few years ago I was training a working group at a medical center. Their manager, who had attended a leadership program based on Nonviolent Communication, contacted us and wanted the group to get more skills on how handle challenging situations.

We did six days of training spread over four months to give the working group training in connection and communication. The aim was for them to be able to use what they learned directly in their work situations.

The content was based on the results of a survey on what they perceived as challenging in their work situations, with patients, employees and managers. The requests that came up were increased ability to listen, to say "no" without feeling bad about it, to handle stress, to be able to set boundaries in a way that did not damage connection, and to manage both their own and others people's anger.

At the beginning we focused on practical training in communication for the thirty people attending. The fifth training session we talked about how our ability to communicate and to meet other people with empathy is largely influenced by the system we operate in. In order to balance the training they had received as individuals and inspire them to think in a broader perspective, we told them the following story.

Imagine that you are standing by a river. Suddenly you see a baby come floating by and you throw yourself into the water in order to save the child.

You have just gotten up out of the river with the baby when you see another two babies come floating by. Luckily, two men are passing by, so you cry out for help. While you throw yourself in the water for one of the babies, one of the two men takes care of the baby you just rescued from the river and the other one throws himself into the river to save the second baby floating by.

Just when you have saved also these two babies, you will see four babies come floating along the river. More adults come to your aid. More and more people get involved in the rescue work. But the number of babies also seems to increase all the time. It is a hard job and you have no time to talk about what might be the reason that the babies end up in the water, because you are devoting all our efforts to save them.

When you are completely exhausted you drop down on the river bank to rest. The question about how the babies are ending up in the river is spinning around in your head. You tell the others that you intend to find out, aware that they will need to work extra hard if you disappear from helping out. They support you and you start running up the river.

Eventually you reach some kind of "station" where the babies are being thrown into the river. You cry out to the people throwing the babies in, "Why are you doing this? You have to stop! They will drown, can't you see?!"

"But we are only doing what we have been told to do," one of them answers. "It's our job," another one says. "Our orders are from the boss," a third one adds.

After trying to convince them to give up their jobs, you give up. It is difficult to find arguments when they explain how they will lose their jobs and how it would jeopardize their families' security. You realize you will have to try to find the boss or someone else to influence this.

After searching for a while, you find the boss. "You have to stop doing this, the babies will freeze to death or drown if you do not stop!" you say in a desperate voice. "We also feel sorry for these children, but all of our business is based on this and without it, people will have no jobs and growth will stall ..."

Here we finished the story and asked for the participants' reflections. Someone expressed relief realizing that she sometimes felt guilty when it was not up to her to influence a situation. Someone else in the group expressed how she recognized the process, and that she felt despair regarding some of the "rules" in the organization that made it really difficult to use the communication training we had done with them:

"How do you think it feels to know that I have no more than two minutes to talk to someone on the phone and that I am supposed to connect to them with empathy?"

We had a emotionally charged discussion, afterwards many of the participants expressing that they had gained valuable insights about responsibility and power.

At our next session with the group, we immediately noticed that there was something going on. For once almost everyone was already gathered in the room we usually met in, and sat and talked in pairs in low, excited voices.

"We have talked," one of them said even before we had time to say "hello." "Talked a lot," said another. "We cannot continue like this, we agree on that. Now we want your help in finding out what we can do."

We were of course curious and asked to hear more.

"However much we learn about communication, we will not be able to do a better job and be less stressed. Rather, it seems to be the case that the more efficient we become at communicating, the faster new babies come floating by."

They agreed that the system they worked in needed some changes to make space for empathy and effective and humane communication. Now they wanted to find out what they could do to influence it. Our three-hour meeting resulted in a long list of what changes they wanted to implement. They decided to invite two senior leaders, who had a lot of power when it came to how their jobs were structured, to a meeting. We practiced how opinions and request could be expressed in that meeting so that they would not sound like threats. We also practiced how they could respond to unwanted replies. They asked at least one of us to join them, as they expressed it, to "stop them" if they did not find a constructive way to express themselves.

The day the meeting took place the atmosphere was charged. During the meeting all kinds of things happened:

Someone ran out of the room, but came back again. Some people talked about things they were really worried about. Another person was crying. In the end the meeting lead to clear discussions about central issues. Together they created concrete ideas and it was the beginning of some important changes in their workplace.

It was exciting to see how individuals and systems now began to interact. The staff's ability to clearly articulate what they felt and needed did lead to completely new results. The system could be adapted to contribute to more people. These changes benefited both those who worked in the system and their patients.

Change often needs to take place both within individuals and within systems to be stable and to hold in the long run. It is not important at which level it starts at, but when it can be made simultaneously on many levels, it has great power.

Chapter 10

"Good Advice" for Different Dilemmas

Here are some dilemmas that may arise in connection situations and how to handle them.

All advice would of course be better, if it was specifically adapted to your situation, but the advice below can hopefully serve as an inspiration when you need it the most.

NOTE! No warranty is promised because life and people are more complex than good advice.

When There are Misunderstandings

When there has been a misunderstanding, there are often different ideas of what has happened. These ideas or perspectives often work as a filter and get in the way of connection, leading people to defend their positions and leading them further and further away from each other. Here are three things you can do to take a step away from misunderstanding:
1. Differentiate interpretations from observations.
2. Listen to what is going on in all parties of the conflict.[1]
3. Shift the focus from "right and wrong" to what everyone involved needs.

When You do not Understand how Others View "Reality"

When we meet someone who has a different view of "reality" than we have, my advice is first and foremost to listen. Listen with the

---

1 Read more about conflicts on page 70 .

attitude of hearing something that you have not previously understood and that you would benefit from understanding.

Try to really understand what is important to the other person. You do not need to agree, just to listen. For the moment, put down all attempts to prove to any one else that you are right and they are wrong – as this will only make it more difficult to connect.

Another way to listen when your reality doesn't fit with someone else's is to focus on the ways you may be able to recognize yourself in the other person. I suggest you try to look for the person's needs – as human needs are a shared place.

When Someone Does Not Tell You The (Whole) Truth

Another situation where it is important how I connect to someone, is when I see "signs" that they have experienced something they have chosen not to talk about. They may be subject to, for example, domestic violence, or have a strong feeling of shame about their own or a relative's abuse. It can be a specific event or something that recurs often. It may be something they have done and are ashamed of, or something that someone close to them has done.[2]

In these circumstances it is, of course, important to listen, but also to be honest with your "suspicions". I want, with vulnerable honesty, without analysis or attacks, to show that I care. This can help the other person dare to open up, either at once, or later. As a start you may say something like this:

"When I listen to you, I notice a concern in myself that I would like to tell you about, would you like to hear?"

If you get a yes, you may continue.

"I became worried when you said you did not want to go to the conference because it will be "such a hullabaloo" when you get home

---

[2] Läs mer om det på sidan 97.

again. I am simply afraid that you are not safe. How is it for you to hear my worries?"

This is a very simplified way to explain a complex situation that is affected by many components. Often, the most challenging part is to get through the feelings of shame and to dare to open up and talk about what is actually going on. You cannot rush this, but it is possible to show that you are willing to listen to what is communicated and that you can hear even that which is not said.

Something I have learned is that it doesn't matter if the person opens up in these situations or not, but it feels good for me not to be passive and silent. It has also happened that while sometimes a person has first denied what I have asked about, they have later come to me again to talk about it after a few weeks.[3]

When Someone Hears Demands

If someone hears what we ask for as a demand, we know that they have missed what we need. It is common for people to hear demands from, for example, the boss or from a person of authority and this may make it harder to create connection.

When someone hears what you say as a demand - try to rephrase what you say. Express as clearly as you can what you want to achieve the things you ask for. Listen to the person and ask if he or she possibly hears what you say as a demand. It can help the person to become aware of that she or he hears your request as a demand, even if you do not actually demand anything.

One thing to listen for, is if the person expresses his or her wish to influence and to make choices of her own. If you notice this, confirm that you hear that this is important for him or her. Remember you do not have to agree to anything just because you listen.

---

3 Read more about this in my book "Anger, guilt and shame: Reclaiming power and choice".

When Someone Hears Criticism

I assume that when people hear what I say as criticism, they have not heard what I need. Therefore, I usually try to rephrase what I have said in these situations. I am careful to avoid mixing in some interpretations regarding the other person's intention, ability or requests in what I say, and instead only say what it is that I want to change and why it is important for me.

If you suspect that someone hears criticism, express what you want to say in small pieces and make sure that each piece is clear before you give the next. A common reason that people hear criticism is that they get more than they can handle, and then it is easy to become defensive.

If someone still hears what you say as criticism, listen and try to understand how this happens. Maybe it comes down to something completely different than you originally thought it was about, so be ready to really take in what the other person is saying. Usual needs when someone hears criticism are respect, acceptance and participation. When you listen, you may realize that your have been less clear than you thought or that you missed some important detail.[4]

When Dialogue is Not Suitable

Although this book is about how we can communicate in different situations, there are times when we will rather terminate or decide not to engage in dialogue. It may be, for example, when we find that we cannot find a way to connect because we are so upset. It may also be in situations we perceive as threatening, or as a waste of time, or in some other way destructive. See more under the heading "Threats" on page 125.

We might want to take a break to have time to think about what we really want. This can preferably be said like this:

"I understand this is very important to you, and I care about that. At

---

[4] Read ore about criticism in Chapter 3 from page 43.

the same time I want to end our conversation for right now because I think it would be more effective for both of us if we have a third person present Can we meet again on Tuesday when I can ask Kim to join us."

If you take a break in the middle of a conversation, it is usually easier for the other person to accept it if you also suggest another possibility for him or her to continue the conversation, either at a different time or with another person.

"I understand that you really yearn for a solution to this and since I do not see how I can help you, I want to ask you to turn to X to be able move on with this. Okay?"

When You Don't Experience Connection

When you do not experience connection, it may be because of a variety of circumstances. One possibility is that people do not understand how important it is for you to get information or to connect. Another is that they do not know how to give you what you need. A third possibility is that people are so busy trying to deal with something that happens within themselves, that they actually do not have the space to take in what you want at that moment.

You can try out variations of the lines below, but be sure to include both that it is important for you to experience more connection, and what they concretely can do for you to experience it.

"I would need to connect some more to be able to understand if what I say is valuable for you to hear. Would you like to tell me how this is for you?"

"I feel worried that we are talking past each other because I am keen that we can resolve this, do you want to tell me how this is for you?"

If no one in the group answers your questions, you can make it easier for them to communicate with you. Remember that many people are afraid to talk in a group.

"I would like to understand if what I say is valuable for you to hear. Would those who would rather shift focus now raise their hands?"

Nonverbal Communication

Sighs, rolling eyes, knocks on the table and other nonverbal communication can be a challenge to manage. Some of us ignore such signals and consider that expressing themselves is solely a person's s own responsibility if there is something they want to say.

Others point out non verbal communication or criticize people for not being direct and honest, even if it is not directed towards them.

I suggest that you say something about what you see but in a way that deepens the connection rather than suggests that someone does something wrong. Allow yourself to be curious and drop all the interpretations you make of others.

Read more about this under "Master suppression techniques" on page xx.

When You Get to Take Over an Old Sourdough

When we meet someone who has been in conflict with one of our colleagues, they may see us as "supporting the other side.". That we are part of an opposing team. Be prepared to be seen through a "colored lens" and to possibly having to put up with being spoken to in a way that might be painful. Refrain from arguing in order to be seen differently. It is your chance to show that the opposing team is an illusion.

Make sure to make a conscious choice before you give them information they have not asked for. At least until you have gained a deeper connection. As so often is it useful to start by listening!

When You Listen to Complaints

If we receive complaints, our reaction will, to a large extent, depend on the way we regard feedback from other people. We can see complaints as an expression of disgruntled people who never are content, or ungrateful and demanding. We can also hear criticism as something wrong with us and that we do not deserve to be treated in a better way.

I suggest you try to listen to complaints with the mind of a child or a beginner at something, and see if you can learn something from the situation. The challenge is to be that open without hearing that there is something wrong with you. When we don't take it personally we can begin to hear what the other person is really trying to say. Perhaps you will become aware of something new, about yourself or the other person. You may not have clarity on the background of the criticism, but only with the one who has been blamed for it. Either way, this is an opportunity to find out what is important for this person. You can begin by reflecting back what you have heard that she or he is unhappy about:

"Do I understand you correctly, that the water in the shower was not hot enough and it's really irritating and you would like it fixed immediately? Was there anything else, that I missed?"

"Is it that you really want me to understand how frustrating it is to you that this matter has taken over a month and still is not resolved? Do you want some clarity on what is going on?"

When You Feel Uncertain on How to Act

When we feel uncertain about how to act in a certain situation it is easy to refer to policies or regulations to appear more certain than we are. If we do not make sure that we first try to connect, it is easy to complicate the connection to the person who wants our help.

Expressions like the one below can serve to create connection:

"From what I understand, this is our policy. I want you to know that I would like to be more confident about whether this applies in this situation or not, but until I know better I want to stick to it, so I do not aggravate anything. Can we be in touch in about three days when I have had the chance to talk to my team?"

When Confidentiality Complicates the Situation

In health care and also many other organizations, there is a strict confidentiality code. Sometimes it is a challenge to honor confidentiality guidelines with integrity. It may lead us to avoid asking for support that would help us deal with a situation more skillfully. My advice is to be clear that I would like support yet also want to honor confidentiality. Work together to find a way that does both.

When someone asks you to reveal something that would violate confidentiality, your no is often accepted if you also express the reason. If he or she still requires information, the first step is to listen to why they want it. Maybe the needs they are trying to meet with the information can be satisfied by other means.

The second step is to see if you can be clearer with the reason to why you do not want to provide the information they are looking for. Abbreviated, it can sound like this:

"I understand that you want this information because you hope it will help you. At the same time, I want to be understood in that I want to protect the person the information is about. If you want this information, maybe you can ask the person concerned, and then let her or him decide?"

When Someone Has a negative Attitude

The first thing I would to is to clarify for myself what is is I hear these people express that makes me think that they are "negative." Although we may think that someone's body language and facial expressions are enough "evidence", they can be expressions, for example, for stress or anxiety. Consider these three points:

1. What exactly do you see the person do? What do you hear him or her say that makes you interpret this person as negative?

2. What do you think is going on in the other person? What might the person be feeling and what needs are activated. Is there something she or he wants to protect by the "negative attitude"?

3. What is going on in you? What are your feelings and needs in relation to how this person is behaving? Is there something you are trying to protect in judging the other as having a "negative attitude"?

When You Are Met By Silence

Trying to communicate and being met with silence can be a big challenge because it makes space for our own fantasies. Notice that you have not heard anything from the person and that you really cannot know why.

Listen to what you think is the cause and use these ideas to connect with what you are feeling and needing. Once you have that connection, you can also take action to meet your needs.

If you want to challenge your ability to empathize, you can try to understand what needs the other person is trying to meet with her or his silence. Consider whether there is any other way that the other person would be able to meet their needs, which at that same time can satisfy yours.

When Information Does Not Get Through

If you experience that someone does not hear your information, although they may loudly ask for it, my advice is to listen, listen, listen.

Listening does not mean you need to be totally silent as this sometimes may seem provocative. Listening can also be active and focused on for example what the other person is interested in or longing for. You can listen to what the other person wants, even if you do not agree with or understand the other person in his or her arguments.

I try to remember to listen so intensely that I prepare to be surprised by what I hear. As listening is "contagious", it is often the best way to help an upset person to eventually be able to listen, or at least calm down enough to take in information.

When Someone is Talking Longer Than You Want to Listen

Many of us have learnt that it is not respectful to interrupt someone who is talking. Actually, sometimes it is more respectful to interrupt than to keep quiet. When, for example, you do not understand what someone wants to say, or why he or she wants to say it and you get so busy trying to sort that out, you can cut in to be able to connect and understand.

You can of course do so by saying something like – "I really want to understand what you are wanting me to get and I would like to tell you what I got so far". If you are bored with the conversation, I see it as more respectful to instead interrupt and ask the person if he or she is willing to change the subject so that you continue to speak about something that interests you both.

When you cut in and tell him or her that you want to change the subject, remember to be as specific as possible about what you want. If you are not clear, it is easy for the other person to receive your message as a signal for them to shut up.

If you forget to end your interruption with a request, it may be difficult for the person you are interrupting to hear anything other than criticism. If they get that you interrupt them to feel more connected and not to silent them they will more easily see your intention. I do not think that anyone likes someone else to pretend that they are interested and are listening when they actually are really bored.

"I want to be sure I understand what you want to say and I am about to lose the thread here. Let me see if I have managed to capture all the details. The first thing I heard was that.... "

To feel more connected to the intention someone has with what they are saying you can interrupt someone with guessing what needs she or he wants to meet by talking about this.

"I'm guessing that what you are talking about is really important for you because you want us to understand all the background of it. Is that so?

Many times, it can be effective to both listen and express oneself:

"I guess you really want to have clarity on what is happening with your case?"

And if you get yes for an answer, you can proceed:

"The information I can give is that this issue will be taken up for discussion tomorrow. You can call me at four o'clock tomorrow afternoon. Does this work for you?

Interrupting in this way, contrary to what you might think often creates more security and trust. I think it's more respectful to carefully interrupt than it is to let someone talk past the point when we are no longer listening to them of some reason.

Long ago I was one of the participants in a project group. One person had not quite found his place in the group. On one occasion, he talked about something he thought we should do. It was quite embarrassing because it was a matter outside our field of work and nobody else was interested. Nobody said anything, but there were a lot of nonverbal communication.

Initially I joined the nonverbal communication but after a while I began to feel ashamed. We actually were ridiculing the person instead of honestly expressing how his proposals affected us, and thus gave him no chance to get clarity. So I interrupted him because I decided that it was more respectful than letting him continue. It was tough for him to hear me at first, but in the end, it served our connection and helped him find his place in the group.

When Our Time is Limited

It may feel uncomfortable to point out that we only have for example ten minutes to talk with someone. When everyone knows the existing time constraints it often serves the conversation. If we have stopped listening because the time is up, we can interrupt a conversation like this:

"I'm too stressed to listen to what you need and I feel torn as I really want to understand it. My bus is leaving in two minutes and I need to pick up the kids at daycare. Can I call you when I'm sitting on the bus or can we continue talking about this tomorrow?"

When It is More Important To Be Heard Than To Resolve The Matter

Listening with empathy for others' feelings and needs is often a valuable gift. Realistically you may not have time or desire to devote to the person who wants to be heard.

A receptionist, who took part in one of our courses, said she believed that in 60 % of the calls she had, the persons would like to have more time to be heard. A large part of her stress was frustration about both wanting to contribute to this and keeping up with her other chores.

Sometimes it saves time to take a pause and really take the time to listen to someone. And sometimes it is a challenge to balance this with our other work and then we can say:

"I'm guessing you would like someone to listen to you and take your matter seriously. Unfortunately, I personally have other things booked now, so I suggest that you book an appointment with X to talk this through, would that work for you?"

When It Does Not Feel Comfortable To Talk About Feelings

In some situations, it is not completely accepted to talk about feelings, even if they lie just beneath the surface and everyone knows that they are there. In this case it can happen that someone starts accusing someone else of different things, as this might be easier than to be open about being sad, scared or disappointed. The less trust I have in that what I think will be accepted, the bigger the risk is that I focus on other people's mistakes.

The use of expressions such as "do you feel ...?" or "I feel ..." when trying to understand someone else can feel awkward or vulnerable to them. If I guess this is how other people might experience putting words to their emotion, I can instead ask them about what they need and want, but skip the question about what they feel. At the same time, I want to be aware of that they may have strong emotions that can greatly influence our communication. Read more about emotions on page xx.

When Faced With Challenging Questions

How you answer questions will affect the connection with others. Many of us dread facing some issues. There may be some specific issues that we find difficult to talk about, or to which we do not have any concrete answers. If I know that a "no" from me will be very hard for the other person as what they are requesting is really important to them this can cause me a lot of tension and thus effect my communication skills.

It many situations people may have a unconscious need to be heard and understood. They may most of all want reassurance that someone is getting how much this situation affects them. In many of these situations it is useful to initially listen just with empathy, or at least make a reflection of what you have heard before you give information. If someone says:

"Why don't you do this in a more efficient way?

You can answer something like this:
"Do you get anxious when you see the way we do this and want to know whether we will be ready in time?

And if the answer is yes, you can continue by telling how it is that you have chosen this particular way of doing something. The guess was a way to connect with what was going on within the other person.

When You Hear Challenging Messages

If you are worried about what others will say about something you have done or not done, make sure to create connection with them when you listen to what they have to say. When you are connected, it will be easier to handle differences and dissent.

Avoid arguing, as it tends to create stronger positioning. Also avoid agreeing, as it can cause problems in the long run. Either listen to try to understand, or express what you would like to do about it. But avoid analyzing the other person or assessing his or her intentions as right or wrong. If necessary, take a pause to reflect before you continue the conversation.

When Someone Gets Defensive

When someone defends him or herself, the focus of the conversation often ends up as a contest to decide who is right and who is wrong. A person who defends him or herself often feels guilt or shame and tries to unburden themselves from the tension and discomfort by blaming someone else. Guilt and shame arise from hearing something that has been said as criticism.

If a conversation is focusing on who has done right and wrong, or on finding a scapegoat when something has got out of hand, I tend to listen very carefully. Then I know that a lot of listening, a big heart and a big dose of empathy usually is the greatest gift. I remind myself that behind the defensive speech there are universal needs. In the long run it is more productive to listen for and connect to those needs. It is almost like being a detective curiously turning every rock to find clues. Some examples:

Someone says:

"It can hardly be my fault, because I did, in fact, not get all the information."

In this case it can help the person to "lower their guard" if you answer:

"Would you like to be seen in how you really have done your best under the circumstances?"

Or when someone says:

"It is not as bad as it looks, why are everybody making such a big deal out of this!"

You can answer:

"Do you want to be seen for your ability to care for this situation? Are you puzzled or worried about the strong reactions people are having?"

When The "Chemistry" is Not Matching

Realistically we have more of a chemical "match" to some people and less to others. However, I have also experienced people using this expression as an excuse to avoid dealing with unpleasant conflicts. These conflicts usually involve far more than "chemistry".

We can do a lot to "match" a person to whom we feel a distance. When we like someone we often imitate that person's body language, tone and voice, which enables even deeper connection. We can consciously match also the people we find it harder to connect with. This does not mean imitate everything they do. It does mean to try and authentically be in resonance with their mood and genuinely make guesses about their universal human needs.

When Someone Does not Seem Willing to Change

Sometimes I get requests to "talk to" staff that is regarded as "change reluctant". Often there are some people who oppose to, for example, organizational changes. In most cases, these are the same people who also protested at the three previous organizational changes in the last two years. I have a hard time saying yes to these requests. I consider if the primary purpose is to "convert" people to the decisions of others who have more structural power. While being open to change is an important quality, changes do not necessarily take all needs into consideration. Sometimes change comes about in a way that is not clear to the very people who are tasked with implementing the changes.

Perhaps they see problems with the changes that have not been considered by "higher ups". These "change reluctant" people may be offering valuable information that will help the organization in the long run. Is there an authentic structure through which they can be fully heard. If nothing else, they might bring in clarity around important needs like stability or reliability when implementing change.

Afterword

It has been surprisingly easy to write this book. Partly because I have been helped by various people who work daily with serving others as their work, partly because I have led courses on the subject for many years. One of the challenges has been that "reality" is much more complex than what can easily be summed up in the examples I have chosen to include in the book. In most cases, I have chosen to start with what each individual usually can influence, even though I know that we often face difficulties because the system is not working optimally.

I hope that I have been able to sow a few seeds that will help you "see the human being" and continue the exploration of what is possible in the connection to others. And remember – professionals practice to prepare for big challenges!

Good Luck!

Liv Larsson

Practice Seeing Beyond Labels and Prejudices

Use the list of emotions on page 166 and the list of needs on page 167 as a support in this exercise.

1. Take a moment to reflect on if there is a person that you have a hard time cooperating with or understand. What kind of labels and analyzes do you have about that person? What kind of judgments do you make of his or her intentions with doing certain things. Allow yourself to become aware of all the analysis and interpretations you make of the person, either positive or negative. Try to censor as little as possible in this stage. Finding them is a way to get clarity about thoughts you have that may lie in the way of connection. NOTE - The labels and judgments are not to be communicated to the other person.

b. In what ways do you think your thoughts affect your contact with the other person?

c. What do you see the other person do, or hear the other say that leads to the labels and judgments? Distinguish what you hear and see from your interpretations of it.

4. What do you feel in that moment? Describe your emotional reactions that you can feel in your body and separate them from the thoughts you have written in paragraph 1. Use the list of feelings on page x for support and inspiration.

5. Let the feelings you found in paragraph 4 guide you to your needs. Use the list of needs on page x for support and inspiration in finding what needs are alive in you in this situation. Distinguish between what you need and what you want someone to do.

EXERCISE

6a. When you think about what you feel and need, is there something you want to ask the other person to do? Say? Do differently?

6b. Is there anything you want to ask yourself or anyone else to do, say or do differently? To be clear about what is going on inside of you is the first step. Now it is also valuable to try to put yourself in what might be going on in the other person, even if you, of course, cannot know for sure. To "walk a mile in their shoes" might help you find the entrances to a well-functioning communication between you.

7a. What labels do you think the other person has of you?

7b. What do you think the other person has seen you do, or heard you say, that led to these labels?

7c. What do you think the other person is feeling in these situations? Use the list of feelings on page 166 for support and inspiration to guess what might be going on inside the other person on an emotional level.

7d. What do you think he or she needs? Use the list of needs on page 167 as support and inspiration.

7e. What do you think could help the other person to get their needs met? What do you think she or he would like you to do, say or do differently?

7f. Is there anything you want to say or do differently after this exploration?

Only when you have reached this point, is it time to approach the other person and communicate about this matter.

EXERCISE

Preparing to Meet a "Difficult Person"

Use a moment to get in touch with what is going on within you in relation to someone you regard as "bothersome" or such. The following questions may make it clear to you whether you will act in a situation or not. The answers can also help you decide if you want to do something on your own or with someone else. Whether you then communicate with the other person or not, it usually feels good to sort out the inner matters.

Choose one person at a time so that it becomes as clear as possible what is going on in you. Write down what you think, feel and need by using the list below.

1. What do you think about this person, except that she or he is bothersome? Capture your thoughts, even if you realize that they do not match reality. Try not to censor. Behind these thoughts is valuable information on how this encounter affects you and what you need. Maybe you want to write down the labels you have put on this person, and again, allow yourself to really capture what your mind says, without censorship.
   Write down any judgments about what she or he is doing wrong and should do differently.

2. In what situations do you start to think that the person is bothersome or make any other assessment of him or her? What observations of the person's behavior do you make when your judgments about him or her are stimulated? Write down as precisely as possible what the person does or says. Unlike in paragraph 1, I suggest you carefully separate what you think about the person from what you actually have seen or heard. If there is anything the person says that bothers you, then quote the person. Write down exactly what she or he said, rather than your opinion about her or him saying that. If it is an action that is bothering you, write down what you see the other person doing, rather than what you think about the action.

3. When you are clear about what has happened, connect with what you feel in these moments. Distinguish your feelings from what the other person is doing. For example, you might feel anxious, but remember that if you use terms like "manipulated" or "attacked", you have got your emotions mixed with what the other person has done that has led to these feelings. The "clearer" the emotions are differentiated from thoughts, the easier it is to get clarity on what you need.

4. When your feelings are clear to you, ask yourself what they can tell you about what you need. If you have separated your emotion from any thoughts about what the other person is doing "to you", it will be easier to find out what you need. Use the needs list on page 167 and remember that what I mean by the word "need" is not linked to a particular person or strategy. It is a positive motivating force in you that is not dependent on any one person doing something specific at a certain time.

EXERCISE

5. What would you like to request from the other person that would give you what you need? Is there anyone else you could ask for the same thing? Do you want to make any requests from yourself, regarding your relationship to this person? Let us now try to "walk in the other person's shoes":

6. When she or he did what you wrote about in paragraph 2, what do you think the person felt and needed? Use the needs list on page 167, and remember that a need is not linked to a particular person or strategy. It is a positive motivational force in the person that you can never fully know, but which you can try to connect to in order to increase your understanding.

7. What do you think the other person may want to request?

8. When you have answered the questions in paragraphs 1-6, ask yourself what you could do or ask others to do, in order to meet all the needs that are now on the table.

What Would I Want to Say "No" to? (but find challenging)

Practicing in advance with situations that are recurring, and that you find challenging or stressful is time well spent. In the beginning, it may feel awkward. We may think that this is something we will just deal with if and when it happens. We can do that, but if you want to become a master at this, training is needed. Even the really big chess masters practice several hours a day in order to stay in top shape.

1. Start by yourself or together with a colleague or workgroup by identifying the situations in which it is difficult or challenging to say "no."
   Write down exactly what is said or done that makes it challenging. For example, perhaps you are concerned that your refusal will raise strong feelings and comments like:
   "Who is your boss?"

   "You are not doing your job!"

   "Do you know how many people you will disappoint by saying "no"?"

   Write down what you worry someone will say, or write something that you have already heard someone say, that you are worried about hearing again. Make observations; either by quoting what you have heard someone say or describing specific behaviors you have seen. Turn all interpretations into observations.

2. Choose a situation you want to start practicing on. Start with the one you are most interested in learning more about.

Continue with the exercise on the next page.

Prepare to deliver a "no"

Think of a "no" you experience as a challenge to express. It can be a "No" to anybody: a customer, a guest, a citizen, a colleague, your boss or anyone else. I suggest however that you choose a person that you care about or a connection you want to keep intact.

1. The first step in saying "no" is to express understanding for the needs that are behind the other person's request. Reflect back what you understand is their wish, need or goal in what they are asking for. Once they have confirmed this, check if something has shifted in you that makes you no longer want to say "no." If you still want to say "no," express yourself by following the steps below.

2. Write down (quote) what the other person has asked for.

3. What needs are you saying yes to – what needs do you want to meet - by saying "no" in this situation? You can use the needs list on page 167. That is:
   What prevents you from saying, "yes," to the request?

4. What needs did the other person want to meet by asking for what she or he did? You can use the needs list on page xx again.

5. Consider both what you need and what the other person needs. Think about what you would like to suggest if you still want to say "no" to the others person's way to meet their needs. You are looking for a strategy that has the potential to meet both your and the other person's needs.

6. Formulate a sentence expressing your "no" - Include your observations (the facts), what you need, and maybe what you feel. End with expressing a connecting request, maybe something like:

"What is your relationship to emotions? Is it easy or not for you to put words to your feelings?"

Remember that this is only the start of the dialogue. While it is valuable that you prepare, you never know how the other person will react to what you say to them.

Next step - how do you handle the response to your "no"?

7. No matter how the person answers, there are at least two ways you can react. You can either listen, then try to understand what feelings and needs have been stirred up in the other person when he or she hears your "no." Or you can express what it is that makes you want to say no and end it by asking:
"What do you need to be able to say yes to what I am asking for?"

Or
"As I understand it, you have a need of X. I have a need of Y ...Can you see a strategy that would meet both out needs?

Prepare For a Situation Based on Expectations and Demands

If we hear demands or expectations, we have lost touch with what we, or other people need. Redirect your focus when you hear demands or criticism and listen for feelings and needs instead.

Here are some of the things to consider if you find yourself hearing demands or expectations.

a. In what situation do you often experience demands? What do you hear the other person do or say?
Choose one specific situation at the time for this exercise and do the exercise as many times as you like.

b. What do you feel when you think about this situation?

c. Which of your needs are not being met in this situation?

d. Which needs does the other person want to meet by doing what she or he does?

e. Is there anything you would like to express to the other person?

I suggest that you chose one of these things or a combination of all of them:

- Express a connecting request. That is, check whether the other person understands how this is for you/how you experience this, and investigate her or his reactions to it.
- Express a clear request for something that is possible for the other person to do, or to say 'yes' or 'no' to. Saying "respect me" is not clear, but "I would like you to go out now and come back and talk to me about this in an hour," is more concrete.

Anger

Becoming angry when someone acts in a way that we do not like, whether it is a customer or an employee, is often precarious. Not because of the anger itself, but because we tend to communicate and act in a way that harms relationships when we are angry. Our brain is "kidnapped" by forces that focus on defensiveness, rather than on understanding and trying to sort out ambiguities.[1]

It is valuable therefore, to learn how to manage our own anger when working with people. Many people connect anger to "setting boundaries," but one does not need to be angry to say "no." On the contrary, we need to have a clear head; which is often not the case when we are angry, to be able to say "no" in a way that maintains contact.

When you are angry - remind yourself that:

1. You are angry because one or some of your needs have not been met.

2. You are angry because you are blaming someone else for not getting what you need and wish for.

3. If you express yourself when you are angry, you risk doing it in a way that ensures that you will not get what you need.[2]

---

1 Goleman, Daniel (1995), Emotional intelligence. Random House USA Inc.

2 These points are from my book "*Anger guilt and shame, Reclaiming Power and Choice*" (2013), Friare Liv.

Six Steps for Dealing with Anger

1. Stop. Breathe. Do or say nothing.

2. Give free space for all judgments, should-thinking and musts, but only WITHOUT saying anything out loud. Observe what is happening within you. Do not censor.

3. Get in touch with your needs behind these judgments, demands or strong feelings. Your anger shows you that there is a forgotten need in you that now is "crying out."

4. Get in touch with what you feel now. Has the feeling shifted? Has the desire to blame or punish the other person changed? Do you want connection to handle the situation in a way that works out for both of you? If you have contact with your needs in such a way, then you are ready to open your mouth.

5. Express your feelings, the needs underneath these feelings and a request for a concrete action or for the other person to reflect back what you have just said.

6. If you cannot connect to what you need, tell the other person that you need some more time to find clarity. Pause and talk with someone else to sort out what is going on.

EXERCISE

List of feeling words

Afraid
Alive
Ambivalent
Angry
Ashamed
Awake
Bored
Calm
Comfortable
Confused
Curious
Delighted
Depressed
Desperate
Disappointed
Disinterested
Downhearted
Embarrassed
Energetic
Enthusiastic
Frustrated
Furious
Gloomy
Grateful
Grumpy
Happy

Hoppful
Impatient
Irritated
Lonely
Moved
Nervous
Overwhelmed
Perplexed
Proud
Restless
Sad
Satisfied
Shocked
Skeptical
Stressed
Sure
Surprised
Suspicious
Tense
Thrilled
Tired
Uncomfortable
Uneasy
Upset
Vulnerable
Worried

List of words for human needs

Acceptance	Integrity
Acknowledgment	Learning
Authenticity	Light
Autonomy	Love
Balance	Meaning
Beauty	Movement
Belonging	Mutuality
Care	Nurturance
Celbration	Order
Choice	Participation
Clarity	Peace
Closeness	Predictability
Communication	Protection
Community	Relaxation
Connection	Respect
Cooperation	Rest, sleep
Creativity	Safety
Ease	Sexual expression
Efficiency	Shared reality
Empathy	Support
Equality	To be seen & heard
Freedom	To contribute
Fun, Play	To mourn
Harmony	Touch
Health	Trust
Honesty	Understanding
Importance	Warmth
Inspiration	

Literature and references

Bauer, Joachim (2007), Varför jag känner som du känner. Intuitiv kommunikation och hemligheten med spegelneuronerna. Natur och kultur.

Bergqvist, Elaine (2008), Härskarteknik. Bokförlaget HörOpp.

Buber, Martin (1994), Jag och du. Dualis.

Covey, Stephen M R (2008), The Speed of trust - the one thing that changes everything. Simon & Schuster.

Ehrenrich, Barbara (2010), Bright-Sided: How Positive Thinking Is Undermining America. Penguin.

Ezra, Emmanuel (2010), Det goda mötet. Norstedts.

Hoffmann & Larsson (2015), Cracking the Communication Code. Illustrated by Vilhelm Nilsson. Friare Liv.

Larsson, Liv (2011), A Helping Hand.

- (2014), The Power of Gratitude! Friare Liv.
- (2012), Anger, Guilt and Shame. Reclaiming Power and Choice.
- (2012), Relationships. Freedom without Distance, Belonging without Control.
- (2009), Led som du lär. Kursledarskap med Nonviolent Communication. ISBN: 978-91-976671-9-7 Friare Liv.

Lerner, Michael (2000), Spirit Matters. Hampton Roads Publ. Company.

Lyubomirsky, Sonja (2009), The How of Happiness.

Rosenberg, Marshall (2015) Nonviolent Communication, a Language for Life.

The Author - Liv Larsson

Liv Larsson has lead trainings since 1992 with everything from conflict resolution to organizational change as a focus. She is a certified Nonviolent Communication trainer with CNVC with her base in Sweden. Larsson is working all over the world leading trainings. She is active as a mediator in different kind of conflicts.

Author of 20 books on communication, conflicts, shame, anger, mediation and much more. The titles in English are:
- A Helping Hand, Mediation with NVC
- Anger, Guilt & Shame - Reclaiming Power and Choice
- Relationships. Freedom without Distance, Connection without Control
- Cracking the Communication Code. 42 Key differentiations. (Co-autored with Katarina Hoffmann)
- The Power of Gratitude

Find out more about Liv Larsson's work.
www.friareliv.se/eng
www.livlarsson.com

www.ingramcontent.com/pod-product-compliance
Lightning Source LLC
Chambersburg PA
CBHW030716250326
R18027900003B/R180279PG41599CBX00004B/1